Press Freedom and the (Crooked) Path Toward Democracy

JOURNALISM AND POLITICAL COMMUNICATION UNBOUND

Series editors: Daniel Kreiss, University of North Carolina
at Chapel Hill, and Nikki Usher, University of San Diego

Journalism and Political Communication Unbound seeks to be a high-profile book series that reaches far beyond the academy to an interested public of policymakers, journalists, public intellectuals, and citizens eager to make sense of contemporary politics and media. "Unbound" in the series title has multiple meanings: It refers to the unbinding of borders between the fields of communication, political communication, and journalism, as well as related disciplines such as political science, sociology, and science and technology studies; it highlights the ways traditional frameworks for scholarship have disintegrated in the wake of changing digital technologies and new social, political, economic, and cultural dynamics; and it reflects the unbinding of media in a hybrid world of flows across mediums.

Other books in the series:

Journalism Research That Matters
Valérie Bélair-Gagnon and Nikki Usher

Reckoning: Journalism's Limits and Possibilities
Candis Callison and Mary Lynn Young

News After Trump: Journalism's Crisis of Relevance in a Changed Media Culture
Matt Carlson, Sue Robinson, and Seth C. Lewis

Borderland: Decolonizing the Words of War
Chrisanthi Giotis

The Politics of Force: Media and the Construction of Police Brutality
Regina Lawrence

Imagined Audiences: How Journalists Perceive and Pursue the Public
Jacob L. Nelson

Pop Culture, Politics, and the News: Entertainment Journalism in the Polarized Media Landscape
Joel Penney

Democracy Lives in Darkness: How and Why People Keep Their Politics a Secret
Emily Van Duyn

Building Theory in Political Communication: The Politics-Media-Politics Approach
Gadi Wolfsfeld, Tamir Sheafer, and Scott Althaus

Press Freedom and the (Crooked) Path Toward Democracy

Lessons From Journalists in East Africa

MEGHAN SOBEL COHEN AND
KAREN MCINTYRE HOPKINSON

OXFORD

UNIVERSITY PRESS

OXFORD
UNIVERSITY PRESS

Oxford University Press is a department of the University of Oxford. It furthers
the University's objective of excellence in research, scholarship, and education
by publishing worldwide. Oxford is a registered trade mark of Oxford University
Press in the UK and certain other countries.

Published in the United States of America by Oxford University Press
198 Madison Avenue, New York, NY 10016, United States of America.

Library of Congress Cataloging-in-Publication Data
Names: Cohen, Meghan Sobel, author. | Hopkinson, Karen McIntyre, author.
Title: Press freedom and the (crooked) path toward democracy :
lessons from journalists in East Africa / Meghan Sobel Cohen and
Karen McIntyre Hopkinson.
Description: New York : Oxford University Press, [2023]. |
Series: Journalism and political communication unbound |
Includes bibliographical references and index.
Identifiers: LCCN 2023011321 (print) | LCCN 2023011322 (ebook) |
ISBN 9780197634219 (paperback) | ISBN 9780197634202 (hardback) |
ISBN 9780197634233 (epub)
Subjects: LCSH: Freedom of the press—Africa, East. | Mass media—Africa, East. |
Journalism—Political aspects—Africa, East. | Mass media—Political
aspects—Africa, East. | Journalistic ethics—Africa, East.
Classification: LCC PN5450.5.E18 C64 2023 (print) | LCC PN5450.5.E18 (ebook) |
DDC 079.67/6—dc23/eng/20230504
LC record available at https://lccn.loc.gov/2023011321
LC ebook record available at https://lccn.loc.gov/2023011322

DOI: 10.1093/oso/9780197634202.001.0001

Paperback printed by Marquis Book Printing, Canada
Hardback printed by Bridgeport National Bindery, Inc., United States of America

Contents

1

Introduction

East Africa Media Histories and Critique of Existing Frameworks

In 1994, so-called journalists in Rwanda broadcasted messages of hate on the radio, convincing individuals to kill their neighbours. The public listened. The news media, led by Hutu extremists loyal to the government, perpetuated the violence by spreading a "kill or be killed" narrative (Kasoma, 1995; Kellow & Steeves, 1998; Mamdani, 1996; Paris, 2004; Specia, 2017; Taylor, 1999). Since the genocide against the Tutsi, the country has seen impressive economic growth (African Development Bank, 2022) as well as improvements in gender equality (Russell, 2022), literacy rates (Central Intelligence Agency, 2019), and infrastructure and technology (International Labour Organization, 2019). The nation has also seen changes to its media landscape with a rise in the number of media houses, including private and online media, but it receives ongoing criticism for a lack of press freedom in the name of genocide prevention and peacekeeping (Bonde et al., 2015; Frère, 2009; Reporters Without Borders, 2020a).

Similar complex relationships exist between governments and media practitioners around the world. In neighbouring Uganda, a civil war in the 1980s, a fight against the Lord's Resistance Army, and a president who has been in office since 1986 have resulted in restrictions on the press (Chibita, 2009; Kimumwe, 2014; Maractho, 2015; Odongo, 2014). Despite those restrictions, in 2017 Freedom House referred to Uganda as "one of the more vibrant media scenes in east and central Africa" (Freedom House, 2017, para. 5–6), and in 2007 Tabaire said, "[Ugandan President Yoweri] Museveni has received international praise for cultivating a 'relatively liberal media climate'" (p. 204). However, the situation has deteriorated in recent years, with Freedom House saying in 2022 that while the media sector "remains vibrant," the ruling party "retains power through the manipulation of state resources, intimidation by security forces, and politicized prosecutions of opposition leaders. Uganda's civil society and independent media sectors suffer from

Press Freedom and the (Crooked) Path Toward Democracy. Meghan Sobel Cohen and Karen McIntyre Hopkinson, Oxford University Press. © Oxford University Press 2023. DOI: 10.1093/oso/9780197634202.003.0001

legal and extralegal harassment and state violence" (Freedom House, 2022b, para. 1).

The nation in East Africa with the most free press is nearby Kenya, which has seen ethnic and political conflict and terrorist attacks, but nothing close to what Rwanda and Uganda have experienced (Chikwanha, 2007). Kenya has a "highly-competitive press scene" that is said to be "the most sophisticated in east Africa" (BBC, 2022, para. 6). Despite the three nations gaining independence around the same time, each country's path has looked different since then, and Kenya is the only one of the three to escape major internal conflict.

The geographic region is home to one of the longest human histories, with some of the earliest human ancestors being documented in the area. For much of its existence, the region has been at the crossroads (literally and figuratively) of exploration, trade, migration, and global politics. East Africa is home to a number of former colonial states, of which many— including Rwanda, Uganda, Kenya, Burundi, and Tanzania—gained independence in the 1960s. Despite independence, Western nations continued to hold immense power in the region, which "meant that the room for manoeuver of African states was severely constrained by the demands of Western government, supranational bodies and global capital" (Pinkney, 2001, p. 2).

In recent years, East Africa has shown some of the fastest economic growth on the continent (African Development Bank, 2020), but wealth disparity and access to essential goods and services remain problems to different extents. Factors such as state affairs, civil society, external interests, ideology, ethnicity, religion, identity, corruption, and neocolonialism, among many others, impact the political landscape of each country and community within the region. Many nation-states in Africa, including those in East Africa, grapple with multiple, often competing, identities. In many instances, individuals identify first and foremost with their ethnic identity, which has wide-reaching impacts on politics and development (Mwakikagile, 2007; Salih & Markakis, 1998). All of these factors fuse together to impact media structures in unique ways. This simultaneously influences policies and development.

Research across African nations has shown that as people gain access to mass media content, they increasingly support democracy and reject authoritarian rule (Bratton et al., 2005). But this ecosystem can be cyclical, as "conditions of war and conflict can stress the political–economic context of media outlets to the point that journalists and their news content become compromised in trying to report neutrally beyond the subtle editorial leanings seen in more peaceful eras" (Lemke, 2020, p. 473).

As such, this book uses the histories, contestations, and political changes occurring in Rwanda, Uganda, and Kenya to examine mediascapes at varying stages of social and political development—Rwanda, which experienced a genocide in 1994, is in relatively early (though fast-paced) stages of reconstruction; Uganda, which experienced a civil war in the 1980s and continued unrest through the 1990s (but arguably not to the extent of Rwanda's genocide), can be considered in a middle stage of development; and Kenya, which has remained largely peaceful, relatively speaking, can be understood as being in a more advanced stage of development.

However, it is important to note that instead of viewing these countries (and the region) as situated within monolithic binaries of developed versus developing or Western versus non-Western or democratic versus non-democratic, we see them as prongs temporarily stationed at various places along a spectrum in which shifting geopolitical relations impact both their situation as well as those in nations around the world. It is the array of events and political changes occurring in these nations that this book highlights.[1] We follow in Voltmer's (2013) footsteps by using Whitehead's "notion of democracy and democratic journalism as 'floating, but anchored' concepts" (Whitehead, 2002, p. 6, as cited in Voltmer, 2013, p. 5). South African media scholar Herman Wasserman (2018) has suggested the idea of "critical global journalism" and, specifically, "critical regionalism" that

> takes into account the varied and multiple ideologies, practices, and institutions of journalisms around the world, yet seeks interconnections and comparisons between them. Instead of treating them as marginal cultural curiosities or, conversely, succumbing to cultural relativism in which different sets of practices are uncritically accepted in the name of diversity, journalisms outside the dominant centers of scholarly production should be engaged with robustly. (p. 121)

It is within the lenses of critical global journalism and "floating, but anchored" democracy and democratic journalism that this book draws on qualitative in-depth interviews and a cross-national survey to examine press freedom and the role of media in development in East Africa. Press freedom, also referred to as media freedom, can be defined as:

The liberty to publish and distribute content on any platform, free from the control, censorship, or harassment of the state. While these repressive measures continue to pose a significant threat, media freedom requires much more than just the absence of censorship—it needs a proactive promotion and protection. (UNESCO, 2021, p. 45)

In addition to offering an updated state of the media in these three countries, this book shows how a nation's political and cultural intricacies complicate traditional media development frameworks and notions of press freedom. Specifically, this book shows that much of the existing media and communication scholarship that has attempted to classify media systems around the world has overlooked the world's developing nations, particularly those in Africa. The scholarship that has focused specifically on developing nations has been constructed largely on a misguided premise that nations develop in a linear fashion—from non-democracy to democracy, and, in doing so, from a restricted press to a free press. In reality, the ebb and flow of political change, democratization, and backsliding calls for more historically informed views of media systems that do not fit into the confines of existing theories. Drawn from conversations with and surveys of journalists in the region, we put forth a new set of factors to consider when aiming to understand media systems in developing nations from a more historically and contextually informed view, including: distance from conflict, benchmarks for political and press freedom change (specifically, who is in office and for how long, elections and their aftermath, political and tribal influences on media ownership, and how laws are interpreted and enforced), international linkages, and the strength of a country's civil society (including nongovernmental organizations, social norms, and journalism cultures).

In the last decade, media freedom has declined in almost all parts of the world (Repucci, 2019), and specifically, "over the last five years, approximately 85% of the world's population have experienced a decline in press freedom in their country" (UNESCO, 2021, p. 15). In East Africa, the results are mixed and debatable. In Rwanda, both international press freedom rankings and journalists on the ground say press freedom has increased in the past 10 years. However, in neighbouring Uganda, both international rankings and local journalists say media freedom has declined. In Kenya, rankings reflect declining freedom over the past decade, but local reporters acknowledge they have more freedom than their counterparts in Uganda and Rwanda. The evolution and current state of press freedom in the region is complex, and we aim to provide an updated and nuanced picture of the topic.

Musa (1997) suggested that to have a "practicable media theory for development, scholars must take into account the historical contexts that gave rise to the present media systems" (p. 143). However, despite decades of calls for historical contexts to be factored into media theories, most still overlook the histories of many nations outside of a select few democratic, Western countries. Weaving together secondary literature and results from original surveys and in-depth interviews with journalists in Rwanda, Uganda, and Kenya, this book examines the impact of an array of social, political, legal, and economic factors on media systems in the region. However, in order to fully understand press freedom and media development, we need to understand media histories. This chapter provides brief discussions of the media histories in each of the three countries, which paint a picture of similarities and differences in the region. The chapter then provides an overview and critique of current theories of media systems as they relate to developing nations. We begin with Rwanda.

Media Landscapes

The Land of a Thousand Hills: News Media in Rwanda[*]

In the years that have followed the genocide, research on Rwanda has grown, with a small number of scholars and activists examining the media ecosystem. While there is not universal agreement about the role of the media in the genocide against the Tutsi (see Straus, 2007), many scholars, activists, and even politicians argue that Rwandan media hold some responsibility for escalating the conflict by "inciting the hatred that led to violence by using an ethnic framework to report what was essentially a political struggle" (Kellow & Steeves, 1998, p. 107) and broadcasting the previously mentioned "kill or be killed" narratives (Kasoma, 1995; Kellow & Steeves, 1998; Mamdani, 1996; Paris, 2004). Others also contend that international media hold some

[*]Portions of this subsection are published in Sobel, M., & McIntyre, K. (2019), The State of Journalism and Press Freedom in Postgenocide Rwanda, *Journalism and Mass Communication Quarterly*, 96(2), 558–578, DOI: 10.1177/1077699018782201; and McIntyre, K., & Sobel, M. (2019), How Rwandan journalists use WhatsApp to Advance Their Profession and Collaborate for the Good of Their Country. *Digital Journalism*, 7(6), 705–724, DOI: 10.1080/21670811.2019.1612261.

responsibility because foreign news coverage was largely absent (Dallaire, 2019; Livingston, 2007), and as the theory of agenda setting argues, media attention to distant crises can trigger policy responses (McCombs & Shaw, 1972). The small amount of international coverage that did focus on the events unfolding did so "by casting it in a formulaic way as anarchic tribal warfare rather than an organized genocide" (Thompson, 2019, p. 2). Mark Doyle (2019), a BBC East Africa correspondent at the time of the genocide against the Tutsi, said this about the lack of international response and coverage: "It was racism, stupid!" (p. 34).

In Rwanda, Radio-Television Libre des Mille Collines (RTLM), a radio station technically independent but run by hard-line Hutu party officials and loyalists, was the primary Rwandan outlet used to broadcast the hateful messages (Bromley, 2007; Kamilindi, 2007; Kellow & Steeves, 1998). RTLM "reporters" dehumanized Tutsi individuals by calling them cockroaches, disclosing their hiding places, and urging Hutus to kill their Tutsi neighbours (Bromley, 2007; Kellow & Steeves, 1998). Similarly, the newspaper *Kangura* is said to have helped brainwash Hutus into thinking they were superior and should eliminate Tutsis by publishing and preaching the infamous Hutu Ten Commandments (Kamilindi, 2007), which asserted that Tutsis were dishonest and therefore could not be trusted in any authoritative position in society, and that Hutus should have no mercy on them. Bromley (2007) described this as a premeditated process of cultural and social exclusion. The international community failed to intervene during the genocide, including a refusal to use radio jamming technology to block RTLM broadcasts (Grzyb, 2019). Yanagizawa-Drott (2014) found that approximately 10% of overall violence, and almost one-third of the violence conducted by militias and other armed groups, can be attributed to RTML's broadcasts.

In order to more fully understand how the media were able to perpetuate the genocide, and why the public largely obeyed their calls to action, it is important to understand the larger media landscape in Rwanda at the time. The news media, as an institution, were new in Rwanda. The first newspaper, published by the Catholic Church, was established in 1933. The government launched a newspaper and radio station in the 1960s, but it was not until the 1990s that the news industry became relatively prevalent. And when it did, the press in Rwanda did not adhere to Western notions of journalistic objectivity. For the most part, news organizations were government owned. RTLM was operated by Hutu-party loyalists and other like-minded people in positions of authority, including military and businessmen, who ascribed to the racist thinking of then-president Juvénal Habyarimana (Kamilindi, 2007). For this reason, many journalists participated in the hate media out of fear for their own lives. There was no space for opposing views—48 journalists who publicly opposed the genocide were killed (Kamilindi, 2007).

Since the genocide, the Rwandan mediascape has changed dramatically. An influx of international donors enabled the number of media houses to grow, and the country's first School of Journalism and Communication was established at the University of Rwanda (originally the National University of Rwanda) in 1995 with the support of UNESCO (Kayumba & Kimonyo, 2006). However, Rwanda's postgenocide government needed to ensure that this expansion of news organizations would not result in hate speech and violence as the country's media had done in the recent past.

Thus, the Rwandan Patriotic Front (RPF), the ruling political party in Rwanda, led by President Paul Kagame, "promoted private media outlets to create a façade of media pluralism" while simultaneously suppressing independent journalism under the veil of inciting ethnic divisionism and perpetuating genocidal ideology (Waldorf, 2007, p. 404). Before 2002, most media outlets in Rwanda were government owned, but the years that followed saw a rapid liberalization of the media, resulting in the country having 39 FM radio stations, 20 TV stations, eight newspapers, and 24 registered news websites as of 2021 (Rwanda Governance Board, 2021).

Although commercial media houses are permitted in Rwanda, the ownership structure of news outlets can be difficult to determine. In a survey of Rwandan journalists, more than one third of respondents said that ownership of media is not transparent in the country (Bonde et al., 2015). Furthermore, many privately owned media houses rely on government-funded advertising, and journalists claim that government entities buy ads from outlets that editorially support the government and withhold advertising revenue from those that are critical (Bonde et al., 2015), thus muddying the distinction between public and private organizations. In addition, media outlets operate under the oversight of the government. For nearly two decades, they were overseen by the Media High Council, created in 2002 as the High Council of the Press, which was said to be an independent body but was "attached to the Presidency of the Republic" (Frère, 2009, p. 343). In early 2021, the Media High Council was phased out and its responsibilities taken over by the Ministry of Local Government (MINALOC) and the Rwanda Governance Board (RGB). Such government oversight blurs the lines of autonomy.

Although the Rwandan mediascape has evolved in many ways since the genocide against the Tutsi, a number of legal and extralegal mechanisms restrict journalists, and international press freedom bodies remain critical. President Kagame maintains tight control over the press, often in the name of preventing another genocide (Frère, 2009; Mudge, 2021), despite critics arguing the opposite—that "opening political space is the best way to *prevent* another genocide" (Kinzer, 2011, para. 9). The press freedom environment in Rwanda, and the accuracy of press freedom rankings and metrics, is brought into question throughout the book, with an explicit discussion in Chapter 2.

The Pearl of Africa: News Media in Uganda[*]

Uganda's mediascape has always been, and still is, inextricably tied to the country's political structure. The first newspapers were seen in the country in the early 1900s, brought by missionaries from the Church Missionary Society (Isoba, 1980). The first privately owned, commercial newspaper, *The Uganda Herald*, was established in Uganda in 1912 and was widely read, especially compared to missionary-run newspapers which focused heavily on church news. It remained the most influential newspaper in the country until the mid-1950s (Isoba, 1980). *Uganda Argus*, a newspaper which would later become owned by the government and is now called *New Vision*, was created in 1955 and provided such strong competition that *The Uganda Herald* went out of business (Isoba, 1980).

Critical journalism is said to have begun in Uganda in 1920 with the "first independent African newspaper," *Sekanyolya*, which criticized both the kingdom and the colonial government (Gariyo, 1993; Lugalambi & Tabaire, 2010, p. 4). In 1949, political turmoil caused riots, and the regime blamed newspapers. The Press Censorship and Publications Act of 1949 was enacted and limited the circulation of several newspapers, which were later banned (Lugalambi & Tabaire, 2010).

By the mid-20th century, the number of media houses had grown rapidly but quickly declined again due to policies that limited the number of newspapers (Isoba, 1980). Uganda endured persistent civil conflict under President Apollo Milton Obote in the 1960s and 1980s and numerous coups

---

*Portions of this subsection are published in Sobel Cohen, M., & McIntyre, K. (2020), The State of Press Freedom in Uganda, *International Journal of Communication*, 14, 649–668.

d'état during President Idi Amin's dictatorial rule in the 1970s, during which free expression was limited. Amin exerted tight government control over the young news industry because he "believed Ugandans were not yet mature enough to think and decide for themselves" (Isoba, 1980, p. 232).

Despite enduring what Mwesige (2004) referred to as "some of the worst political and economic chaos anywhere in the world" (p. 71), for the last quarter-century the country has seen improvements to its media sector under Museveni (Kalyango & Eckler, 2010). When Museveni declared himself president in 1986, he promised a free press. The number of media houses skyrocketed, and journalists enjoyed more freedom than ever before. Even government-run newspapers broke news about corruption scandals involving government officials (Tripp, 2004). By the 1990s the broadcast sector experienced widespread liberalization, and in 1995 further opened under a new national constitution.

The Ugandan media environment is now home to multiple daily newspapers. Government-owned *Bukedde*, the Luganda-language daily, is the highest circulated with just over 33,000 print copies per day, followed by the government-owned *New Vision*, which has a circulation of approximately 23,600 copies per day, and the independent paper *Daily Monitor*, with a circulation around 16,000 (Uganda Business News, 2020). Weekly papers such as *The East African*, *The Weekly Observer*, and *Sunrise* also exist alongside more than 30 TV channels and more than 200 licensed radio stations (BBC Media Action, 2019; Uganda Communications Commission, 2020). Uganda remains ethnologically diverse with more than three dozen languages in usage. The nation's official languages are English and, as of July 2022, Swahili (Kagonye, 2022), but most national media broadcast in English or Luganda, with many local languages spoken on regional radio (BBC Media Action, 2019).

Similar to many other nations, Uganda's media are primarily owned by a small number of large corporations. Such concentration "creates a big barrier to new entrants in the industry . . . and media content is targeted at meeting the interests of advertisers, instead of the 'public interest'" (Nassanga, 2009, pp. 121–122). Participatory radio programs have grown as a means of filling that gap and serving community interests (Nassanga, 2009).

Overall, a picture is likely emerging that shows how the history of the media sector in Uganda can be understood as a continuous back-and-forth between the government and publishers, in which periods of vibrant media growth are followed immediately by periods of substantial state crackdowns, and this has been the case since the 1920s (Stremlau, 2018). Chibita and Fourie (2007) explained that the Ugandan government has a long history of suppressing citizen participation in governance and free expression largely due to "bad colonial and postcolonial policies on the media and language, poverty, low levels of education, and lack of basic access to the means of participation" (p. 2). Regulations are also unevenly distributed among media houses because many owners of commercial media houses hold substantial financial and political power, and some self-censor to ensure that their outlets do not offend the government (Chibita, 2009).

Additionally, the government continues to directly restrict media freedoms. It is not uncommon for the government to detain journalists or temporarily shut down media houses. Reporters and editors are charged with sedition, treason, defamation, and other vaguely written laws whenever they become too critical of the administration (Kalyango & Eckler, 2010; Mwesige, 2004). And journalists who are not formally charged regularly deal with threats, intimidation, and violence from government officials (Reporters Without Borders, 2020b). Unsurprisingly, this has resulted in ongoing self-censorship (Dicklitch & Lwanga, 2003).

Apart from government interference, several other factors have thwarted Uganda's media industry since its inception, including limited foreign investment, a lack of formal journalism training, and inadequate resources (Isoba, 1980). The lack of sufficient training coupled with poor pay leads to unprofessional behaviour, including journalists accepting bribes, working with the government to spy on colleagues reporting critical stories, and tailoring editorial content to meet the interests of advertisers (McIntyre & Sobel Cohen, 2019; Nassanga, 2009).

Despite these challenges, Ugandan journalists are said to be undergoing a process of "journalistic domestication" in which there are "growing pains, but ultimately, Ugandan journalists are working through a difficult procedure of establishing their own journalistic norms and professional practices" (Sobel Cohen & McIntyre, 2020a, p. 666). As mentioned, Uganda's mediascape "remains vibrant" (Freedom House, 2022b, para. 6), and "Museveni has received international praise for cultivating a 'relatively liberal media climate'" (Tabaire, 2007, p. 204).

However, much of the discussion about the liberalized media environment stems from the large number of private media organizations in the country rather than journalists' ability to report freely. Critics say that, as a semi-authoritarian state, Uganda's ruling party implements just enough democratic policies to appear democratic, and thus to appease international donors, but ultimately aims to limit freedoms in order to stay in power—an ecosystem called a safety valve. The safety valve is a political science framework that explains a situation in which journalists and citizens are given just enough space for freedom of expression that they feel as if they are able to air their grievances, and thus they continue on, but no changes occur to the existing social and political structures (Buehler, 2013; MacKinnon, 2008; Sobel Cohen & McIntyre, 2020a). There are ongoing discussions, some led by renowned Ugandan law professor Frederick Jjuuko, for the need for self-regulation in the Ugandan media industry. As Jjuuko (2015) argues, it is unconstitutional for the government to require journalists to have university degrees, belong to a professional body, and/or be licensed in order to undertake what is a fundamental human right.

The Gateway to East Africa: News Media in Kenya[*]

News media began to operate in Kenya in the late 1800s, with Christian missionaries operating publications with a primary goal of spreading biblical teachings (Ugangu, 2016). These missionary-based publications were followed by a colonial press which was primarily managed by settlers to promote their ways and means (Ugangu, 2016). In the 1920s the nation saw the creation of new local publications that focused on Kenyan communities and were published in local languages (Abuoga & Mutere, 1988). "Gradually, as the clamour for independence gathered momentum in the 1940s, so did indigenous African publications. These publications mostly served as platforms for preaching and spreading the liberation gospel while simultaneously expressing grievances of African peoples" (Ugangu, 2016, p. 13). Many of these publications ended up shutting down rather quickly, but they provided space for colonized people to voice their opinions and laid important groundwork for future publications and media spaces (Abuoga & Mutere, 1988). Publications that supported the independence movements then emerged and helped advance the push for independence (Mbeke, 2010).

---

[*]Portions of this subsection are published in Sobel Cohen, M., & McIntyre, K. (2020), Local-language radio stations in Kenya: Helpful or harmful? *African Journalism Studies*, 40(3), 73–88.

The Kenya News Agency (KNA) was created in 1963, the same year that Kenya declared independence from Britain (Hachten, 1965). KNA's predecessor was the Kenya Information Service, which was established in the country in 1939 to convey information about World War II (though it stopped operating when the war ended) (Kenya News Agency, n.d.). At the time, KNA exclusively provided news for the *Voice of Kenya*, which were the government-owned radio and television programs, resulting in what Hachten (1965) called "monotony and dullness that comes with long reading of government pronouncements" (p. 263). Back then there were an estimated 350,000 to 500,000 radio sets (mostly transistors) in the country, which made it the most popular platform (Hachten, 1965). Fast-forward to present times and, according to its website, KNA is "the flagship of the Department of Information" (Kenya News Agency, n.d., para. 1).

Alongside KNA, today Kenya has a diverse and "highly-competitive" media environment (BBC, 2022, para. 6). Despite its vibrancy, much like mediascapes around the world, the industry has faced challenges with professionalism (Obonyo, 2003), holding itself accountable (Obonyo, 2021), and declining revenues (Harwood et al., 2018), among others, including government restrictions imposed on the press in the name of national security (Reporters Without Borders, 2019).

Scholars have well documented the complex relationship between politics and the press throughout Kenyan history, as people with political and economic influence have controlled the media for their personal and ideological benefit (Ambala, 2014). As a result, politicians and those in their spheres of influence are consistently portrayed as heroes in a top-heavy structure where "state heroes" create "grand narratives" (Ambala, 2016, p. 50) rather than everyday people having a say in the stories about their communities (Ogola, 2011a). Ambala (2016) referred to the Kenyan mediascape as one constituted by " 'tribal' hegemony in media ownership" in which the violence that took place after the 2007 election

revealed, more than ever before, that certain voices and narratives were privileged over others from a "tribal" perspective. The overwhelming dominance of the "big" tribe communities in broadcasting, at the exclusion of "smaller" communities, deprives the latter of an equitable "voice" and representation in the national television broadcasting space. (p. 59)

Citizens and activists have tried to alter the existing top-down media structure. A convergence culture—one in which grassroots, consumer-driven initiatives exist side by side with top-down corporate projects (Jenkins, 2006)—could be at play in the digital media arena in Kenya (Ambala, 2016), which would allow for a more balanced and representative set of voices to be heard (Thumim, 2012) and which have been shown to play a role in nation-building by providing a space for ongoing conversation (Ambala, 2016).

In addition to grassroots community media, vernacular radio—radio stations that broadcast news and entertainment in indigenous languages (Sang, 2015)—serve important functions. Kenya has two official languages—Swahili (or Kiswahili), which an estimated 17 million Kenyans speak with some level of proficiency (Doochin, 2019), and English, which is "the language of prestige purposes" and was inherited from British colonizers (Githiora, 2008, p. 236). However, in a nation with dozens of tribes, many communities speak their own language, and before the growth of vernacular radio stations, access to information in these community languages was limited to informal community networks or media content from the state-run broadcaster Kenya Broadcasting Corporation (KBC) (Ismail & Deane, 2008).

Vernacular stations are different from traditional community radio stations, though, because "commercial incentives, rather than development or political ones, drove the opening of these stations. The majority of the new stations were founded as profit-making enterprises" (Ismail & Deane, 2008, p. 322). Originally, vernacular radio stations primarily served music and entertainment purposes, but in response to audience demand, many now air talk shows and phone-in programs which serve as forums for public debate (Ismail & Deane, 2008). There are now more than 30 vernacular stations in varying regions around the country (Sang, 2015), and, as of 2007, these local-language radio stations held 27% of the radio market (BBC Monitoring Database, 2008, as cited in Ismail & Deane, 2008).

After contested election results were announced in December of 2007, vernacular stations were blamed for fueling the anger that led to violence by broadcasting implicit and explicit violence-inducing messages (Ismail & Deane, 2008). In Kenya today, vernacular stations play many positive roles by preserving culture and tribal histories and promoting development and political participation, but can also be seen as propaganda based on the beliefs of the station's owner and have led to tribal divisions (Sobel Cohen & McIntyre, 2020b). However, Kenyans have many choices about what media they consume, so they are not limited to vernacular radio. As we mentioned, Kenya has one of the most developed and liberalized media systems in the region, which could be a precursor to or a result of the nation's political structures.

Theories of Media Systems

As discussed earlier in this chapter, research has shown linkages between access to mass media content and growing support for democracy (Bratton et al., 2005). As such, an array of scholars have attempted to theorize relationships among media, development, and democracy. A growing number of theoretical frameworks have been created to examine and understand media systems around the world, but qualitatively and quantitatively, the field has fallen short of wholly accounting for nations of varying developmental and democratic statuses. Most frameworks, in general, overlook the particularities of developing nations and thus lack applicability to large portions of the world.

Siebert et al.'s (1956) *Four Theories of the Press* introduced four theories classifying the world's presses—authoritarian, libertarian, social responsibility, and Soviet communist—and has been an influential piece of scholarship on comparative press systems and normative media theories for decades. However, critics have noted some of the book's shortcomings: It omitted non-Western and nonliberal epistemologies and practices; it overlooked complex factors such as race, class, gender, and ethnicity; and communities undergoing significant development transitions often lack the infrastructure, financial resources, and professional skills to sustain media institutions similar to those in the developed world (Altschull, 1984; Hachten, 1981; McQuail, 1983; Nerone, 2018).

Hallin and Mancini's (2004) book *Comparing Media Systems: Three Models of Media and Politics* uses four dimensions to compare cases/countries—the structure of media markets, the degree and form of political parallelism, journalistic professionalism, and the role of the state—within which they proposed three models of media systems: Mediterranean or polarized pluralist, North/Central European or democratic corporatist, and the North Atlantic or liberal model. These models stem from Western European and North American cases and, despite some scholars attempting to fit varying African nations into the polarized pluralist model due to a strong role of the state and limited professionalism among journalists (Hadland, 2010), many, including Hallin and Mancini, acknowledge that these models do not apply to developing nations. In an attempt to depart from this bias towards mature democracies, Hallin and Mancini (2012) followed up with *Comparing Media Systems: Beyond the Western World*, an edited volume that has been a seminal piece of work but which features only one chapter about an African nation and it is South Africa, the most developed nation on the continent and the one with a media system relatively similar to developed, Western countries. Even that chapter explains, "South Africa is a poor fit for any of the three models, a square peg faced by three round holes," and that "Africa has a contribution to make to the Hallin–Mancini hypothesis and that fertile ground exists for the design of an alternative model or models populated by the experiences and dynamics of postcolonial African democracies" (Hadland, 2012, pp. 111–112). Voltmer's (2012) chapter in the book explains that the polarized pluralist model has essentially become a catch-all for nations that do not fit into the other categories. In many instances this is vastly inaccurate, and Voltmer (2012) explains the difficulty in classifying media systems in non-democratic countries and transitional democracies, and calls for an expansion of categories beyond those suggested by Hallin and Mancini (2012).

Without trying to put forth a theory of media systems, Weaver's (1998) *Global Journalist* book is an expansive, comparative cross-national study examining journalists in 21 countries or territories, with one African nation—the North African country of Algeria. Weaver and Willnat's (2012) follow-up book, *The Global Journalist in the 21st Century*, is an edited volume with sections focused on journalism cultures in Asia, Australia and New Zealand, Europe, North America, South America, and the Middle East, but no section about Africa. One chapter in the 585-page book is a comparative study of 18 nations, of which two, Uganda and Egypt, are on the African continent (Hanitzsch et al., 2012). But this data was not part of the Global Journalist project; it came from the Worlds of Journalism Study (Hanitzsch et al., 2019). In sum, we find little representation of Africa in global journalism research.

Here's the problem: When media research overlooks developing nations, specifically those in Africa, we misunderstand key elements of media systems—namely, how they function in unique ways in nations at different levels of political and economic spectrums. The hegemonic epistemological assumptions on which much existing work is based are grounded in Western thought. This Western way of thinking contributes to a cycle that perpetuates misunderstandings about non-Western media systems.

For example, Western perspectives might ignore the African moral philosophy of *ubuntu*, which has been defined and applied a number of different ways, but means "humanness" or "humanity" and has been commonly translated to mean "I am because we are" (Bujo, 2001; Gyekye, 1987; Masolo, 2004; Mokgoro, 1998). The idea of ubuntu is rooted in Southern African cultures and essentially means that people and communities are inherently bound together and defines self-realization in terms of communal and harmonious relationships with others, and the ability to exhibit solidarity with them (Metz, 2011; Metz & Gaie, 2010). "In such places as Rwanda, Burundi and Uganda, the concept [of ubuntu] has other shades of interpretation, such as 'human generosity'" (Matupire, 2017, p. 10). In Rwanda specifically, ubuntu philosophy has been central in many post-genocide reconciliation efforts, including in the Gacaca system of restorative justice (de Beer, 2019; Hinton, 2015).

Linkages between ubuntu and journalism practices have been explored, primarily by Western and South African scholars, in the context of journalism ethics or underlying ethos of reporting (see, e.g., Blankenberg, 1999; Chasi & Rodny-Gumede, 2021; Christians, 2000, 2004; Ess, 2013; Fourie, 2011; Mboti, 2015; Metz, 2015; Rao & Wasserman, 2007; Rodny-Gumede, 2015; Tomaselli, 2011; Wasserman, 2013, 2018). While ubuntu may not be widespread in East Africa, the concept could apply. When journalists are critical of their governments, it can be interpreted as opposing development aims and acting contrary to national or communal values. Obviously, this poses challenges such as privacy (Ess, 2013), individual rights (Blankenberg, 1999; Tomaselli, 2011), and freedom of speech (Metz, 2015) when conceptualizing ubuntu journalism cultures or media systems within this perspective.

> If African philosophies of personhood and agency stress interdependence between the individual and the community and between communities, and if journalists each identify with any of the many cultural communities seeking recognition and representation at local and national levels, they are bound to be torn between serving their communities and serving the "imagined" rights-bearing, autonomous individual "citizen" of the liberal democratic model. (Nyamnjoh, 2005, p. 28)

That is not to say that all media scholarship, or even all African media scholarship, should be grounded in ubuntu philosophies, but theories created without values salient in varying regions (in this case, e.g., grounded in relational or communal values that are more prominent in sub-Saharan belief systems) will be ineffective. This can be seen in the inapplicability of many of the normative theories of the press developed in the West.

We are certainly not the first to note this disconnect. Many, including Hanitzsch et al. (2012), have called this out: "Journalism researchers often focused on Western countries at the expense of other world regions, most notably Africa, Latin America, and parts of Asia," they say. And thus, "concepts and theories that underpinned much of the research primarily originated from the West and were not necessarily suited to non-Western contexts" (p. 473).

Similarly, Chasi and Rodny-Gumede (2021) explain:

> Much journalism, locally [within Africa] as well as internationally is still shaped by ideas as well as practices emanating from decidedly "Western" normative ideas of journalism that leaves little room for exploring alternative models of practices as well as the underlying ethos of reporting. This is also emphasized through postcolonial theory that has deliberated on, and critiqued, the normative ideas around media function/s, media performance and ethics entrenched in Western philosophical belief systems essentially ignoring non-Western philosophical ideas on how the media should or could function in society. (p. 20)

As a result of this visible gap, a growing body of work has emerged that seeks to understand and include media systems in developing countries, largely in response to the *Four Theories*. In 1981, Hachten suggested five normative concepts of the press: authoritarian, Western, Communist, revolutionary, and developmental. After the collapse of the Soviet Union, Hachten (1992) altered that typology to include only four dimensions: authoritarian, Western, revolutionary, and developmental. The developmental concept, as discussed in both of Hachten's frameworks, "emerged in the wake of political independence in impoverished nations throughout the developing world" and suggests that media should promote nation-building and "support authority, not challenge it" (Hachten & Scotton, 2012, p. 40). The developmental concept shares traits with the authoritarian concept, particularly with top-down information flows and situations in which press freedom can be restricted based on the development aims of the ruling party (Hachten, 1981, 1996). Similarly, older attempts were made to classify global media systems in part based on developmental statuses similar to first, second, and third world: market or Western nations, Marxist or communitarian nations, and advancing or developing nations (Altschull, 1984) and Western, Communist, and third world (Martin & Chaudhary, 1983).

Media development theory (also called development media theory) is another framework created with low- and middle-income nations in mind. Media development theory posits that media freedom, while desirable, should be subordinated to the political, economic, social, and cultural needs of the country to promote development (McQuail, 1983). With the exception of the Communist perspective, capitalism was legitimized in the classical *Four Theories*, but under development media theory, the media undertook the role of carrying out positive social change programs, even if that meant accepting restrictions from the government (McQuail, 1983, 2010). McQuail (2010) put it bluntly: "Social responsibility comes before media rights and freedoms" (p. 151). Critics suggest that this idea promotes government propaganda and that media should never willingly give up the ability to criticize government policies even if it risks causing those policies to fail (Hachten & Scotton, 2012).

Derived from development media theory is the centralized mass media method, which calls for government and media to work together to distribute a general message to a wide audience, but this method creates the message in a top-down fashion without considering the public's opinions or desires (Moemeka, 1991). This method is used in most developing countries, especially in Africa, because it is cheap and easy, and it is generally effective in delivering a message to a specific intended audience. However, it has not always been successful in getting individuals to understand and accept the message and act accordingly (Moemeka, 1991).

Nisbet and Moehler (2005) and Voltmer (2013) have, arguably, proposed the most Africa-centric frameworks. Nisbet and Moehler (2005) suggested five political communication models that could apply to nations in sub-Saharan Africa—open democratic, liberalized democratic, liberalized autocratic, closed autocratic, and repressive autocratic—based on the type of political regime and the level of press freedom and amount of legal, political, and economic control that governments exert over media organizations. These five models provide a solid foundation to build from and, taken in conjunction with other media systems frameworks, provide the field's most nuanced focus on the Global South, but as we explain in the following chapters, much of this work tends to take a universalistic approach to the press that does not account for transitions and change. The lived experiences of journalists are complicated and fluid and do not easily align with one political demarcation. It has been suggested that some emerging democracies are moving in a different direction than the liberal model of the Western world and will end up functioning in a new hybrid democracy and will feature hybrid forms of journalism (Voltmer, 2013). Thus, we need to consider history and politics more holistically, as journalists may at times work in conjunction with and at times navigate around the changing social and political dynamics that continuously occur in their countries and around the world.

In a similar way of moving beyond Western-centric notions of media systems in developed democracies, and likely most applicable to this book, is Voltmer's *The Media in Transitional Democracies*. Voltmer (2013) builds on Hallin and Mancini's (2004) four dimensions of modern media systems to suggest four arenas—political, economic, social, and professional—that influence the development of independent press systems in transitional democracies. Voltmer (2013) explains that "arguably, the key arena of democratizing the media is concerned with the reconfiguration of the relationship between the media and the state" (p. 133) and that "democracy and a free press are only possible in a functioning state" (p. 224), so all important state institutions, government, parliament, and the judiciary need to create the environment for media freedom to exist. Following the importance of relationships between media and the state is the economy of the media industry, in which, Voltmer (2013) argues, "commercial media are not necessarily independent media. What is needed are mechanisms of ownership transparency and rules to curb the political power of media ownership, which is far more difficult to achieve than simply privatizing the media industry" (p. 225). Then the framework turns to relationships between media and group interests and ideological divisions: Building from Seymore-Ure's (1974) conceptualization of "press-party parallelism"—that being the ways and degree in which media systems mirror political party systems in a country—and Hallin and Mancini's (2004) notion of "political parallelism" which accounts for media alliances with all forms of political groups (not just political parties) and is related to the idea of external diversity which is when a media outlet promotes a specific viewpoint and ignores or dismisses opposing perspectives, Voltmer (2013) argues that "political parallelism plays an important role in democratic politics. But the mobilizing power of partisanship can easily turn into destructive forces that spread intolerance and even hatred between groups of citizens," and, ultimately, that "building democracy in post-conflict societies poses particular problems and dilemmas to issues of press freedom and political parallelism that defy easy and clear-cut solutions" (p. 180). Lastly, Voltmer's (2013) framework includes journalistic professionalism, in which she argues that journalism as a profession changes after operating under authoritarianism, and new forms of journalism are created with vastly different political, social, and economic norms (and can result in unethical behaviours by journalists such as accepting bribes/being paid for positive coverage); this is where the previously mentioned hybrid forms of journalism come into play.

> Essential to the transformation of journalism is the adoption of new professional ethics and performance norms to ensure that the media fulfill their democratic roles. Media assistance organizations usually expect journalists to adopt the Anglo-Saxon model of journalism that emphasizes political detachment and adversarialism. However, many journalists in emerging democracies argue that this model does not sufficiently take into account the particular social and political circumstances of their countries. As a response, various alternative models of journalism have emerged, amongst others so-called development journalism. Indigenous forms of journalism help the media to respond to audience needs, but they may also serve as an excuse for complacency about existing social hierarchies. (Voltmer, 2013, pp. 226–227)

While Voltmer's (2013) proposed arenas are useful, they leave open much space for ambiguity when it comes to measurement. In other words, what are we looking for within each of those arenas to understand how a specific media system functions?

Thinking more narrowly about press freedom, Ibelema et al. (2000) assert that most existing press system classifications are too rigid. The forces that push towards more press freedom are constantly fighting the forces pushing for more control, and thus, press freedom is not static. Ibelema et al. (2000) put forth seven factors which contribute to press freedom and press control ("two simultaneously acting forces" [p. 110])—the first five can either facilitate press control or enhance press freedom, while the last two largely promote media freedom:

- Structural: "conditions in a given society that may limit or expand people's options. Such conditions include economic status and opportunities, diversity in media ownership, and educational opportunities" (p. 103).

- Political: "the realities of power distribution and the process of governance in a given society . . . much of what is traditionally classified as censorship, as well as the actions of vigilante groups, political thugs, and even death squads" (p. 104).
- Cultural: "the value systems at any given place that consigns everybody's behavior within that context" (p. 106).
- Relational/managerial: "human relations processes that facilitate the accomplishments of one's objectives with the other" (p. 107).
- Technological: "the growth of portable and stealthy technologies of mass communication" (p. 108).
- Semantic: "the human capacity to convey information in subtle ways and to take advantage of inherent ambiguity and contradictions of language" (p. 109).
- Existentialist: "When all else fails, journalists sometimes openly defy restrictions and assert their right to disseminate information . . . Such instances of courage and self-sacrifice are a factor of the logistics of press freedom" (p. 110).

Based on these seven logistical factors, Ibelema et al. (2000) propose the logistical model, which includes four categories to characterize a country's press freedom. When both forces of freedom and forces of control are strong, the press system "tends toward conflict." When both forces are weak, the press system "tends toward apathy." When forces of freedom are strong and forces of control are weak, the press system "tends toward freedom of expression." And when the forces of freedom are weak and the forces of control are strong, the press system "tends toward controlled expression" (p. 111). Ibelema et al.'s (2000) model feels a touch hypocritical because they criticize other classification systems for being too rigid, yet they propose four boxes/categories within which a nation's media system can fit. However, they acknowledge that "the conditions they represent are intended to be seen as continuums rather [than] discrete groups" (p. 112). Their model is one of the more useful in helping to understand press freedom, and a particular strength is that it allows for nonlinear shifts (i.e., a country can move from more freedom to less) and it has been utilized to examine mediascapes in Africa. For example, Fielder and Frère (2018) utilized Ibelema et al.'s (2000) model to examine the media systems in three post-conflict states, Burundi, Rwanda, and the Democratic Republic of Congo, and concluded that political interference, financial issues, difficult working conditions, technical challenges, and journalists' self-perceptions most influence journalists but that, ultimately, one needs to "take into account specific sub-factors that are not included in the analysis of media structures in the Western world" (p. 139).

Overall, much of this existing work can be connected to the broad idea of development journalism, which is said to be "one of the defining normative frameworks within which journalists in Africa have understood their role" (Wasserman, 2018, p. 91). The concept of development journalism arose in Asia, but gained traction in other regions. In Africa, this genre of journalism grew in popularity in the 1970s and 1980s alongside the New World Information and Communication Order debates which sought to reorient global media flows. Governments of multiple African nations formally adopted media policies based on development journalism as a means of collaboration between governments and media for the purpose of social and national growth (Christians et al., 2009; Domatob & Hall, 1983). Critics say that this resulted in a lack of critical reporting and a suppression of the media in the name of nation-building (Kunczik, 1988; Ochs, 1986; Xu, 2009). Attempts at reconceptualizing development journalism have emerged in recent years, including Banda's (2007) suggestions that development journalism should be based on ideologies of public service broadcasting, where audiences are viewed as citizens rather than consumers and engaged participants in problem identification and resolution. In some ways, these frameworks resemble social responsibility theory—that publishers operate their media "with some concern for the public good" (Siebert et al., 1956, p. 77)—but in reality, governments have historically used development media for their own aims, which may or may not promote social good.

Similarly, many of these paradigms or schema could, in varying ways, relate to the notion of media development. It has been argued that "the conceptualization of 'media development' is marred by a conflation of means and ends, lack of definition and permeation by narrow normative views" and "can benefit from greater conceptual and analytical clarity" (Berger, 2010, p. 561). Musa (1997) said that development media theory was "at a toddler stage" and "marked by ambiguities and contradictions" (p. 144).

Such criticisms are not lost on media development theorists. Hachten and Scotton (2012) wrote that, as of the mid-1990s, the developmental concept "appeared to be losing momentum" as a result of "current global trends toward more democracy and market economies" which tend to support Western notions of the press (p. 42), and McQuail has worked to develop more applicable normative theories of the media (Christians et al., 2009). However, despite acknowledgment of the criticisms, little has changed with regard to the creation of a "practicable media theory for development" since Musa's (1997, p. 143) call for such a framework. However, as the following chapters demonstrate, maybe the reason that none of the existing frameworks aptly apply is that the particularities of each nation fluctuate in unique ways that may allow a certain theory to apply in one specific moment in time, but not in the moments that follow.

It has been argued that much existing research on classifying media systems "only implicitly touches upon the concept of press freedom" (Fielder & Frère, 2018, pp. 119–120). While it may not be a conscious addition to these existing frameworks, especially because many do not thoroughly interrogate press freedom as a component of media systems, these models tend to presume that press freedom and democracy come hand in hand in a linear, forward-moving progression alongside development. This criticism has been previously noted; for example, in a review of Voltmer's (2013) *The Media in Transitional Democracies*, Run (2014) says that one of the book's weaknesses is that "[political] transitions here are assumed to be trending toward democracy, even when this is not necessarily the case" (p. 199). Without directly stating so, many of these frameworks imply there are certain states of existence or moments in time, but ultimately the media development landscape moves forward alongside linear democratization—that a society moves through various stages of autocratic rule towards democratization, from non-democracy to democracy (or, in accordance with Nisbet and Moehler's [2005] framework: repressive autocratic, to closed autocratic, to liberalized autocratic, to liberalized democratic, to open democratic). And with that progression comes increasingly more press freedom. We believe it is important to put the spotlight on the linear assumption that underpins much of the field's media systems work to show that many nations do not function in such a linear manner. In reality, the ebb and flow of political change, democratization, and backsliding calls for more historically informed views of media systems that do not fit into the confines of existing theories. In other words, a nation may or may not experience more democratization as it sees social, economic, and infrastructure development, and, relatedly but distinct, the country's media may or may not receive more freedoms as this development and/or democratization occurs. Press freedom and media development mean different things in different countries and within different contexts, making it difficult for any theory to aptly apply.

New Considerations for Understanding Press Freedom and Media Development

The following chapters provide an updated state of the media in Rwanda, Uganda, and Kenya and show how each nation's political and cultural intricacies complicate traditional media systems frameworks that have primarily been premised on forward-moving, linear democratization, assuming that news media transition from not free to free. By taking a historically informed view of these countries, we see how the large and small components of political change, which both move a country towards democratization and slide it away, do not fit into the confines of existing theories. Others scholars have noted that press freedom is perceived differently between nations (Voltmer & Wasserman, 2014; Hanitzsch, 2011), so in this book we attempt to build on those notions by showcasing how press freedom manifests itself in three varying East African nations.

Ultimately, in her book (2013) and in her chapter in Hallin and Mancini's book (2012), Voltmer shows that classifying media systems in transitional democracies is incredibly difficult to do. While we fully agree with this, and that complexity is part of what this book demonstrates, we also aim to push forward Voltmer's four arenas by operationalizing them in practical ways. Voltmer's work focuses on "dimensions [that] capture the multiple challenges involved in transforming the media into democratic institutions" (p. 224), and while we are less interested in democratizing the media, these dimensions can be viewed in other ways. We build on these dimensions, or arenas as Voltmer (2013) calls them, to put forward specific factors that can apply to former authoritarian nations, as her work has focused on, as well as current nations experiencing various forms of authoritarian control. In other words, we offer factors that should be considered when examining media systems, and attempting to classify them, in nations across the political spectrum.

So, after diving into the media landscapes of Rwanda, Uganda, and Kenya, we then put forth a number of considerations for understanding media systems outside of the Western world by showing how each individual country's political and historical context is central to understanding its mediascape, which includes its degree of press freedom, development, and democratization. Rather than proposing a uniquely African-centric model in which only African nations can situate themselves, our proposed considerations relate to global media systems and aim to add dimensions to existing frameworks such that they can help explain the changes occurring in a wide array of nations, but with special consideration given to low- and middle-income nations.

As Zelizer (2005) argues, journalistic conventions, routines, and practices are dynamic and contingent on situational and historical circumstances. Nyamnjoh (2005) further explains that almost everywhere liberal democratic assumptions have been made about the media and their role in democratization and society, they have been done with little regard to the cultures, histories, and sociology of African societies. Similarly, Musa (1997) suggests that in order to have a "practicable media theory for development, scholars must take into account the historical contexts that gave rise to the present media systems" (p. 143). Yet, despite decades of calls for historical contexts to be factored into media theories, most still overlook the histories of many developing nations, particularly (and conveniently) as those histories relate to colonization. Further, African media practice must not be construed as homogeneous, as each unique African nation sways in changing directions independently and within and around other nations in the region and the world, and these changes continually influence media structures. Time is not linear, so in addition to time and distance from conflict, current political events or context, such as new elections, growing space for dissent, renewed political or post-election violence, linkages with other nations, and other factors must be considered, as they can impact press freedom and democracy, either by jolting it forward or yanking it back.

In the broadest sense, this book aims to challenge Western notions of press freedom and point to factors that need to be considered when understanding media development and press freedom in developing nations. The following chapters use examples from Rwanda, Uganda, and Kenya to show how existing media systems frameworks are insufficient and overlook essential elements of development, such as distance from conflict, political contexts and fluctuations, and linkages to Western nations, which directly impact a nation's mediascape.

The remainder of the book proceeds in five chapters. Chapter 2 uses Rwanda as a case study to examine a nation that appears to be on a linear, upward trajectory in terms of press freedom, development, and democracy since the 1994 genocide against the Tutsi. After all, the country has made remarkable strides economically and socially since its civil war. However, in that chapter we show that while the assumption of linear democratization is currently at play, that trend might reverse direction in the future.

Chapters 3 and 4 examine the historical and current factors influencing media systems in Uganda and Kenya, respectively, providing an in-depth analysis of current press freedom levels in the two countries and highlighting the ways in which each country's history, contestations, and political influencers impact its media system. Specifically, we show how changes, or a lack of change, in political leadership has impacted press freedoms, development, and democracy in nonlinear ways.

Chapter 5 examines specific factors—political and development-related events, processes, or structures—that journalists in East Africa say impact their freedoms, but could also apply in other parts of the world. Chapter 5 dissects the ways these changes relate to democratization and the structure of a nation's media system and shows how certain events or systems can promote, slow, alter, or derail development and democratization, in turn improving or lessening levels of press freedom.

Chapter 6, the concluding chapter, revisits the questions of how free the press is in each of these three nations, by what measures, and with what implications for development and democratization. The chapter makes a call for the field to reconsider the use and applicability of existing frameworks, instead looking more comprehensively at how and why a country's media may function in the ways that they do (perhaps with some or all of the factors put forward in Chapter 5).

The appendix features a detailed explanation of our methodology.

Note

1. Similar to other political science scholars, such as Pinkney (2001), this book uses the terms "the West" and "Western" in their political rather than geographic sense to point to wealthy nations that operate liberal democracies and free market economies. The Associated Press Stylebook suggests using "developing nations/world" to refer to economically developing nations of Africa, Asia, and Latin America. Others have argued that the developing–developed typology merely replaced the colonized–colonizer relationship and that "global South" has similar negative connotations by focusing on poor countries in the southern hemisphere (Silver, 2015). Given that we focus primarily on nations' media systems in this book, we use a variety of terminology, including economic status, "Western," "developed/developing," and "global South." We understand the criticisms of each and do not use these terms lightly, but instead use them in various capacities to point to geographic, political, and economic variances that impact media systems.

2

Rwanda

A Linear Progression Toward Press Freedom and Democracy?

As a result of the not-so-distant genocide and the news media's role in perpetuating it, understanding the levels of press freedom and democratization in Rwanda today can be exceptionally complex. The state of press freedom in the country is perceived differently by outsiders than by those within Rwanda, with insiders lamenting that outsiders fail to consider the country's history and unique complexities. In this chapter, we argue that indeed the country's history—and the 1994 genocide against the Tutsi specifically—should be at the forefront of consideration when understanding and evaluating press freedom in the nation. We describe competing perceptions of press freedom in Rwanda and then discuss major political, social, cultural, and economic factors that have influenced the evolution of such freedoms over the last three decades. This chapter argues that McQuail's (1983) theory of media development and Hachten's (1981, 1996) developmental concept—that media should support nation-building and support authority, not challenge it, and that media freedom takes a backseat to governmental aims during development—may be working in the short term, but in the long term may reinforce existing authoritarian power structures in Rwanda. This chapter is part of a larger effort to argue that although a positive relationship appears to exist between a country's distance from civil war and its degree of press freedom (longer period of peace equals more press freedom), as can be seen on first glance in East Africa, development and democratization are not linear, and each nation's contextual factors must be considered when evaluating press freedom.

Press Freedom and the (Crooked) Path Toward Democracy. Meghan Sobel Cohen and Karen McIntyre Hopkinson, Oxford University Press. © Oxford University Press 2023. DOI: 10.1093/oso/9780197634202.003.0002

Perceptions of Press Freedom

Outsiders' Perspective

Although its news media landscape has developed significantly since the genocide against the Tutsi, Rwanda is still regarded as a nation with an oppressed media sector, at least from the outside looking in. International press freedom bodies have consistently published critical evaluations of the country. Reporters Without Borders ranked Rwanda 136th out of 180 countries on the 2022 World Press Freedom Index (with 180 representing the least free country) (Reporters Without Borders, 2022c), and Freedom House ranked Rwanda "not free" in its 2022 report (Freedom House, 2022a). While the Reporters Without Borders ranking has improved in recent years— up from, for example, 162 in 2014 (Reporters Without Borders, 2014)—it continues to categorize Rwanda as home to a great deal of media control. In evaluating press freedom, these entities consider, in part, the number of journalists killed, detained, reported missing, or pressured to flee the country; the obstacles foreign journalists face trying to report in or on the country; laws used to restrict the news media; the political system in place that results in both direct government censorship as well as indirect self-censorship; and economic constraints linked to media ownership (Reporters Without Borders, 2022b). Such rankings have been criticized for a lack of transparency in their methods, biases in their underlying assumptions, unclear conceptual bases, and tendency to examine press freedom from a Western perspective (Becker et al., 2007; Schneider, 2014; Sobel & McIntyre, 2019). However, these independent evaluations are critical, both because they are used by international bodies to help determine the allocation of development aid and because nations (like those in this study) that guarantee press freedom in their legal documents do not necessarily provide such freedoms in reality (Breunig, 1994, as cited in Becker et al., 2007). Becker and colleagues (2007) evaluated four well-known organizations that measure the concept—the International Research and Exchanges Board (IREX), Reporters sans Frontières/Reporters Without Borders (RSF), Committee to Protect Journalists (CPJ), and Freedom House—and found that these entities seemed to measure press freedom in similar ways (Becker et at., 2007).

Various organizations track the number of journalists who have been killed, disappeared, or fled. Reporters Without Borders (2022c) claimed that eight journalists had been killed or reported missing and 35 had been pressured to flee Rwanda since 1996. The Committee to Protect Journalists (2022) reported 17 journalists murdered (15 of those during the genocide against the Tutsi), 12 imprisoned, and two missing since 1992. The situation has improved in recent years, although investigative journalist John Williams Ntwali died under unclear circumstances in January 2023. Rwandan police said Ntwali died in a motorbike accident, but with no police report or other details released, Human Rights Watch called for an independent and international investigation to determine if the journalist was murdered (Human Rights Watch, 2023). The next most recent recorded death of a journalist was Jean Léonard Rugambage in 2010; the editor was shot dead in front of his house reportedly months after the government had shut down the print publication of his newspaper due to its critical coverage of the government (BBC, 2010; Committee to Protect Journalists, 2022). The Rwandan government has shut down both domestic and foreign media houses for broadcasting coverage it did not approve of; it forbade the BBC from publishing its Kinyarwanda (the country's official language) news service in the country in 2014 after the international news outlet aired a documentary that questioned the official narrative surrounding the 1994 genocide against the Tutsi (Rhodes, 2014). Similarly, the Rwandan government reportedly forced a U.S.-based radio station broadcasting religious sermons in Rwanda to shut down after revoking its license due to a presenter referring to women as evil (Amah, 2018). President Kagame is accused of creating such a severe culture of fear that if critics, including journalists, are not killed, they are silenced by the fear that they live in (Sundaram, 2016).

Murder and mandatory shutdowns, however, are not the most common forms of media oppression in Rwanda. Journalists are more often censored either directly or indirectly under the veil of maintaining peace and security in the country. As Reporters Without Borders (2022c) put it, "The memory of the genocide and hate media . . . is widely exploited to prevent the expression of any dissent or criticism" (para. 3). Certain laws used to restrict journalists, discussed in this chapter, are used in conjunction with less formal policies and completely informal, sometimes intangible modes of socialization and control that are used by the government to keep journalists towing the party line. At least that is how the international community tends to see it.

Insiders' Perspective*

Overall, international reporters, NGOs, and academic scholars identify Rwanda as a country with low levels of press freedom. However, our qualitative and quantitative research revealed that journalists working in Rwanda paint a different picture. In 2019, at the time of our survey, Rwanda was ranked 155th out of 179 in the Reporters Without Borders Press Freedom Index. Figure 2.1 shows that those journalists largely did not agree with that ranking.

In our survey, journalists in Rwanda ($n = 174$) rated their country's level of press freedom as an average of 61.29 on a scale from 1 to 100 with 100 reflecting the most freedom. Although they indicated that this is less freedom than they would prefer to have (88.98), they also said they felt they had more freedom than international rankings reflect and significantly more freedom than they had 25 years ago (43.33). See Figure 2.2.

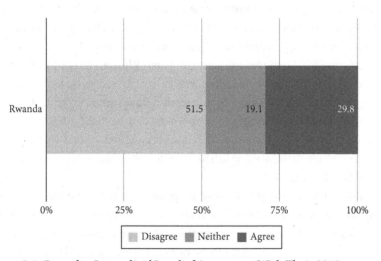

Figure 2.1 Rwandan Journalists' Level of Agreement With Their 2019 Reporters Without Borders Press Freedom Ranking

*Portions of this chapter were published in Sobel, M., & McIntyre, K. (2019), The State of Journalism and Press Freedom in Postgenocide Rwanda, *Journalism and Mass Communication Quarterly*, 96(2), 558–578; McIntyre, K., & Sobel, M. (2019), How Rwandan Journalists Use WhatsApp to Advance Their Profession and Collaborate for the Good of Their Country, *Digital Journalism*, 7(6), 705–724; and Sobel, M., & McIntyre, K. (2018), Journalists' Perceptions of Human Rights Reporting in Rwanda, *African Journalism Studies*, 39(3), 85–104.

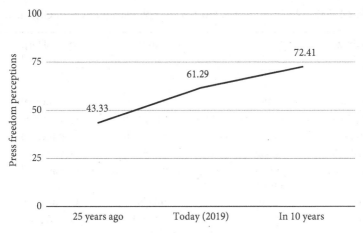

Figure 2.2 Rwandan Journalists' Perceived Level of Press Freedom Over Time
Note. 0 = no freedom; 100 = full freedom.

Further, of the 24 journalists we interviewed (listed in Table 2.1), the majority felt they had quite a bit of freedom and that global press freedom indices are inaccurate at worst and misleading at best because they do not consider the context of the country's history.

A Rwanda-based news editor from *The East African*, an independent news outlet, called Rwanda's global press freedom rankings "disturbing," indicating that reporters in the country have more freedom than the rankings reflect (Journalist 17, personal communication, June 1, 2016). A reporter in Kigali working for the Associated Press said, "People from outside, they think the media in Rwanda is very terrible . . . but there has been some progress" (Journalist 18, personal communication, June 1, 2016). And a Kigali-based reporter who asked that we withhold the name of their employer suggested that people visit the country before criticizing the media landscape or ranking the level of press freedom: "I would like them to come and do re-search and to know why media is [the way that it currently is]" (Journalist 7, personal communication, June 5, 2016).

Overall, the journalists we interviewed said they feel they can report freely and the level of press freedom is constantly improving. Journalists said reg-ulatory bodies, academic institutions, and professional organizations have been created to promote and protect press freedom in the country's post-genocide era, including the Media High Council (which has since become defunct, but whose responsibilities have been taken over by the Ministry

Table 2.1 Rwanda: Interviewee, Job Title, Employer, and Type of Organization

Participant	Job Title	Employer	Type of Org.
Journalist 1	Former radio/TV presenter	Voice of Africa*	Religious
Journalist 2	Editor	Radio/TV 10	Commercial
Journalist 3	Online news editor	Izuba Rirashe	Government
Journalist 4	Senior producer	Radio/TV 10	Commercial
Journalist 5	Former journalist	Withheld	Government
Journalist 6	Editor/reporter/presenter	Radio Isango Star	Commercial
Journalist 7	Reporter	Withheld	Commercial
Journalist 8	Reporter	The New Times	Gov./Commercial
Journalist 9	Editor	Umusingi	Commercial
Journalist 10	Management role	Umuseke.rw	Commercial
Journalist 11	Journalist	Royal FM	Commercial
Journalist 12	Reporter	The New Times	Gov./Commercial
Journalist 13	Editor	Gusenga.org	Religious
Journalist 14	Senior reporter	Izuba Rirashe	Government
Journalist 15	Reporter	City Radio	Commercial
Journalist 16	Freelancer	The New Times	Gov./Commercial
Journalist 17	News editor	The East African*	Commercial
Journalist 18	Reporter	Associated Press*	Commercial
Journalist 19	Former journalist	Withheld	Government
Journalist 20	Management role	Radio Salus	Student
Journalist 21	Reporter	Radio Salus	Student
Journalist 22	Reporter	Kigali Today/KT Radio	Commercial
Journalist 23	Management role	Great Lakes Voice	Commercial
Journalist 24	Editor	Kigali Today	Commercial

* Foreign news outlet (not headquartered in the country where the interview occurred)

of Local Government and the Rwanda Governance Board), the University of Rwanda School of Journalism and Communication, and the Association of Rwandan Journalists. Reporters and editors said they feel free to report openly on many topics and that they play a watchdog role, among other roles, holding the powerful accountable.

However, despite journalists saying that they play many roles, including a watchdog role, they simultaneously explained how they work with the government and limit their content (especially their criticism of the government) based on government guidelines. For example, a reporter in a management role at the commercial outlet Umuseke explained that they need to report critically *and* positively about the government:

> There are some changing mindsets with top officials, even the president . . . some [government officials] change [their minds to understand] that we [journalists] have to be here and we have to be critical and we have to be positive. We have to be both. We have to be balanced. (Journalist 10, personal communication, May 30, 2016)

At times, what the journalists described as media freedom resembled what outsiders would likely consider media restrictions. A senior producer from the commercial station Radio/TV 10 highlighted this by explaining:

> You are free to say what you want depending on the topic and depending on the history of our country. That's, I can't say that we are free or we are not free. It depends on what you want to talk about and when you want to talk about [it] and who you are talking to. (Journalist 4, personal communication, May 28, 2016)

Similarly, a reporter at the student-run Radio Salus based in Huye/Butare, Rwanda, reiterated similar ideas, saying:

> The level of press freedom here—in entertainment and sports it's high. . . . But on other subjects, especially politics, human rights, no, it's very low. It's very low. For instance, talking about genocide issues, they [the government] want only one version of the story. . . . You can't do a balanced story with that. (Journalist 21, personal communication, June 2, 2016)

Despite feeling relatively free, journalists in Rwanda are undeniably restricted in the topics they are allowed to openly cover. Most notably, controversial politics are a no-go. Criticizing the president has landed journalists in jail in the past (Amnesty International, 2010; Noorlander, 2010). More recently, the Supreme Court of Rwanda decriminalized the use of "words, gestures, writings, or cartoons to humiliate members of parliament, members of the cabinet, security officers, or any other public servant" including the president (U.S. Department of State, 2021, para. 67). However, it is unclear if this decriminalization is respected, as other vaguely worded laws still repress dissent (Human Rights Watch, 2022). Stories about the genocide and reunification efforts are delicate, especially when it comes to ethnicity. Rwandans are not to be identified as members of ethnic groups such as Hutu or Tutsi; instead, everyone is Rwandan (Lacey, 2004).

But what became clear in our interviews is that journalists in Rwanda feel as if they are free because they know how to report things in ways that work around government restrictions. A reporter from *The New Times*, which claims to be independent but is regarded as the largest government-run newspaper in the country due to its ideological leaning and government funding, said, "I want to believe that we have actually a majority of the say in whatever we cover. Maybe the difference would be in what light we cover [it]" (Journalist 8, personal communication, May 29, 2016). Similarly, a former radio and TV presenter from Voice of Africa in Rwanda said:

[Journalists] know how to speak. . . . That's the way many journalists know how to [work within the restrictions]. [They] know the way to speak things, the way to write things. 'Cause if you have [*sic*] the way, I think you can talk about anything you want, even the dangerous issues. You can talk about them [dangerous issues], but that's what you're gonna use, the way you're gonna pronounce it, the way you're gonna ask questions. (Journalist 1, personal communication, May 21, 2016)

Ethnicity is one example of a no-go topic where journalists navigate around government restrictions in order to write about it. The news editor that we previously quoted from *The East African* explained:

Quite often you omit [controversial issues] in your work . . . especially issues around ethnicity. You might cover an issue, but you may not be able to explore the different angles around it because you may find yourself, you know, difficulty with the law. So we don't have specific off limits—you can't cover this, you can't, no—but there are some provisions within the law. For instance, like, within the penal code, I think it's article 701, it has this clause on media offenses that could lead to public disorder or insecurity, you know, incite, but it does not specify exactly what. So what that means is you always are trying to say, "Okay, how can I cover the issue and I don't incite?" (Journalist 17, personal communication, June 1, 2016)

The journalists' perceptions of press freedom were relative, and they cannot be considered without context. *The East African* news editor further said:

> We cannot say we operate with the same level of independence as, for instance, our other counterparts in the region, Uganda or Kenya. And again it's because of the history. There are certain sensitivities around how you cover issues. . . . So to that extent, when you're doing your work, that sort of guides you and at the same time limits [you]. (Journalist 17, personal communication, June 1, 2016)

Evolution of Press Freedom: Historical, Political, Cultural Context

Individuals and organizations from Western countries tend to perceive the level of media freedom in Rwanda to be low when compared to media systems in their own developed democracies and other, more democratic nations in the region. However, from a Rwandan perspective, media freedom has improved significantly in the past 30 years, allowing for an optimistic outlook. The state of press freedom in Rwanda is not easily deemed "free" or "not free"; instead, it is fluid and contextual—outsiders focus on the problems that remain while insiders focus on the progress that has been made.

The disconnect between insiders' and outsiders' perceptions of such freedom can be understood, in part, by looking at the country's history. Our survey data revealed that Rwandan journalists rated national laws, fear of government retaliation, and self-censorship as the biggest factors influencing press freedom in the country (see Table 3.3). These restrictions placed on media houses, and the resulting fear, are inextricably linked to the 1994 genocide against the Tutsi and the professional and cultural norms, social and economic policies, and political leadership that came afterward. Our fieldwork made it clear that these major factors have influenced press freedom in the country. Thus, it is important that a country's history, and specifically its temporal distance from civil conflict, should be considered when studying press freedom, and although Rwanda's progression has been relatively linear since the genocide against the Tutsi, that steady climb toward democracy might not last. (As the next two chapters will show, ultimately the progression of a country's democracy is not linear.)

Political History Sets the Stage

One cannot begin to understand the Rwandan political or media land-scape, let alone the complexities of press freedom in the country, without—at minimum—a basic understanding of the nation's history and the 1994 genocide against the Tutsi, which still permeates many aspects of Rwandan society. Hutus settled as farmers in the Great Lakes region of Central and Eastern Africa between 500 and 1000 BC, and Tutsis arrived later as cattle herders, which often placed them in a position of economic dominance and resulted in decades of tension (Des Forges, 1999; Záhořík, 2012). In many ways, Hutus and Tutsis were similar—they shared common histories, a language, a religion, and cultural traits—and did not appear to be simply "ethnic" or "racial" groups; instead, more accurately, they were categorized by occupation or social status (Mamdani, 2001). Such simplistic thinking re-garding racial or ethnic categorization is not unique to Rwanda and is com-monplace across Africa.

> The study of the African realities has for too long been seen in terms of tribes. Whatever happens in Kenya, Uganda, Malawi is because of Tribe A versus Tribe B. Whatever erupts in Zaire, Nigeria, Liberia, Zambia is because of the traditional enmity between Tribe D and Tribe C. . . . This misleading stock interpretation of the African realities has been popularized by the western media which likes to deflect people from seeing that imperialism is still the root cause of many problems in Africa. (wa Thiong'o, 1986, p. 1)

Specifically in Rwanda, the politicization of the Hutu and Tutsi began in the second half of the nineteenth century when a reorganization of the land (then provinces of German East Africa called "Ruanda-Urundi"—now Rwanda and Burundi) placed a great deal of centralized power with the then-king (Mamdani, 2001). The impact of colonial rule, first by Germany and after World War I by Belgium, cannot be understated, as colonial practices and ideologies exacerbated these differences and turned what were essen-tially economic differences into groups focused on ethnicity (Nardone, 2010). Shea (2002) explains:

> The Tutsi were the closest in resemblance to the Europeans. A small ruling class of Tutsi were not only beautiful by European standards, but also rich and powerful. The resemblance consisted in the sometimes similar physical

structure to Europeans and the comparable social status of the Tutsi ruling class. These characteristics were important to the German and Belgian colonizers who were looking for the easiest way to gain control of the area. The Tutsi, though in the minority, were the most highly placed members of society in the area. Belgium viewed the arrangement of the Tutsi minority as rulers through the lens of the popular science of the day. It was, according to such theories, an arrangement orchestrated by nature; rulers are superior by nature to those they rule over. As the Belgians sought to gain control of the Rwandan people they employed the methods thought to be most effective. Through a process of categorization they could quantify and qualify the very being of individual people. The Belgians implemented this plan to gain control beginning in 1926. At that time each person in Rwanda was issued an identity card stating which ethnic group she or he belonged to. (p. 143)

This practice continued in the country until the 1990s. Záhořík (2012) termed this "artificial ethnic categorization" (p. 145).

Fast-forward to April 6, 1994, when a plane carrying Rwandan President Juvénal Habyarimana and Burundian President Cyprien Ntaryamira crashed under still-debated circumstances (Ssuuna, 2016). Existing tensions came to a head and this plane crash sparked a 100-day killing spree that left up to one million Rwandans dead and more than two million refugees (Center for Conflict Management of the National University of Rwanda, 2012). It is worth noting that the number of casualties remains debated, with estimates ranging primarily from 500,000 to one million (Verpoorten, 2005). More recent research suggests that the number of people killed was less than one million (Meierhenrich, 2020) and, specifically, closer to 500,000 (McDoom, 2020). Nsengumukiza (2022) noted that, "The only number that the newly created MINUBUMWE (Ministry of National Unity & Civic Engagement) want media to report is 'over 1,000,000', and not complying with this number is a serious crime with grounds for prosecution" (para. 43). Much of the killing was carried out by civilian Hutus against civilian Tutsis. The genocide against the Tutsi ended when the Rwandan Patriotic Front (RPF), led by Rwanda's current president Paul Kagame, defeated the government-backed militias that spearheaded the killings. The RPF and Kagame remain in control today.

Commemorations take place each year, called Kwibuka—the word for "remember" in Kinyarwanda—and in 2018 the United Nations General

Assembly adopted the phrase *genocide against the Tutsi in Rwanda* in place of *genocide in Rwanda* to leave "no room for ambiguity" (United Nations, 2018, para. 3). Thus, this book uses the phrase *genocide against the Tutsi* to refer to the atrocities that took place in the country in 1994.

Understanding this political history, and the ways in which the genocide against the Tutsi still impact society, is crucial for accurately understanding how and why the Rwandan mediascape functions in the ways that it does. For example, one journalist in Rwanda anonymously said:

> During the genocide commemoration period (Kwibuka), I take a leave of absence because I avoid reporting that can put me in danger, as even the terminology regarding the genocide changes every day. Making any slight mistake even involuntarily lands you in prison. You can be accused of the crime of genocide ideology, one of the most severe crimes we have in Rwanda. To avoid all of that I take a leave, and I stay away from the microphone so I don't fall into the trap. The Kwibuka period is one of the most fearful periods for Rwandan journalists. (Nsengumukiza, 2022, para. 38)

Laws Resulting From the Genocide Restrict Journalists

As the anonymous journalist above alluded to, one of the most blatant ways press freedom today is limited in Rwanda is through legal mechanisms. Although Rwanda's constitution states that "freedom of the press and freedom of information are recognized and guaranteed by the state" (Republic of Rwanda, 2003, Article 34), a number of clauses allow for restrictions and censorship. Vaguely worded laws on libel, insult, contempt for the head of state, or publishing "falsehoods" (Noorlander, 2010) repress journalists, but in talking with journalists about laws that restrict them, the two mentioned most often are a direct result of the 1994 genocide against the Tutsi.

One broadly defined law restricts reporters from generating conflict. This law on divisionism is defined as "a crime committed by any oral or written expression or any act of division that could generate conflicts among the population or cause disputes" (Republic of Rwanda, 2001, Article 3) and is widely applied and commonly used to restrict journalists (Bonde et al., 2015). Specifically, journalists cannot publish anything regarding the relationship between Hutus and Tutsis, and have been warned by government officials to "monitor [online] comments that may imply or call for divisionism"

(Iribagiza, 2022, para. 2). In fact, an editor at the Kinyarwanda-language paper *Umusingi* was arrested and jailed for a year on the charge of inciting divisionism in an opinion column published in June 2012. This editor said, "Why did they imprison me? Because of journalism? . . . Being a journalist is a profession like other professions, it's not a crime" (Journalist 9, personal communication, May 29, 2016).

A law on genocide denial can similarly be used to restrict journalists. This law, passed in 2008, "aims at preventing and punishing the crime of genocide ideology," which is defined as follows:

> An aggregate of thoughts characterized by conduct, speeches, documents and other acts aiming at exterminating or inciting others to exterminate people basing on ethnic group, origin, nationality, region, color, physical appearance, sex, language, religion or political opinion, committed in normal periods or during war. (Republic of Rwanda, 2008, Article 2)

A former journalist in Rwanda who asked us to withhold their employer's name explained that reporters can get creative with their coverage to work around some restrictions, but not when it comes to genocide denial. "Make sure that, you *never*, like, you avoid something that will lead to denial, denial of the genocide" (Journalist 5, personal communication, May 28, 2016). The law further describes various degrees of an act of genocide ideology that range from intimidating or degrading someone to killing them. Individuals convicted of committing this crime in public, as would likely be the case with a journalist, can be sentenced to 20 to 25 years in prison and fined 2 million to 5 million Rwandan francs (roughly 2,000–5,000 USD).

Journalists View Their Roles as Unifiers, Self-Censor

Despite laws being created as a result of the genocide that prevent journalists from reporting freely, the reporters and editors we interviewed agreed that the bulk of media censorship in the country is self-imposed, not government mandated. For example, as mentioned, it is illegal to refer to the Hutu or Tutsi ethnic groups in Rwanda. However, an editor at *The East African* explained that their newspaper self-censors when it comes to discussions about ethnicity not because it is illegal but because journalists in Rwanda feel it is their duty to promote unity and reconciliation: "We feel that if you say 'Rwandan,' whether Hutu or Tutsi, you're helping to address the issue of society looking at one side. . . . So in our coverage, we try not to, you know, highlight ethnicity" (Journalist 17, personal communication, June 1, 2016).

Since the genocide against the Tutsi, the Rwandan government has prioritized development, reconstruction, and unity. Because of their history and shared desire for peace, the role of journalists in present-day Rwanda is tightly interwoven with that of the government; they work together to promote unity. Rwandan journalists believe they should not be autonomous but rather "should operate within constraints from other social institutions" (Moon, 2021, p. 798). Results from our 2019 survey support our interview findings and solidify this point. When asked to rate their agreement that each of 22 professional roles (such as getting information to the public quickly, providing entertainment, discussing international policy, etc.) was a core function of journalism, the journalists gave the lowest rating to the role of serving as a critic of the government. Contrarily, they agreed most with the role of contributing to society's well-being. They also highly rated their roles to support official policies to bring about prosperity and development and to alert the public to potential opportunities.[1]

Our interviews revealed that journalists in Rwanda genuinely want peace in their society; they understand the high stakes of civil conflict (and the news media's role in it), since such conflict occurred so recently that either they or their immediate family members lived through it. To keep the peace, journalists, no matter whether they work for independent or public media houses, regularly self-censor.

A producer at the commercial media house Radio/TV 10 explained:

> Because we are still in a fragile period—you know, it's almost 22 years after [the] genocide . . . and people are still having fresh wounds in their hearts . . . even if we are having developments in Rwanda . . . people who committed genocide are still there; people who suffered are still there; widows, orphans are still there. They are still having a fresh memory. They are still having fresh wounds. It means that we have to be careful. Because of that, some people do self-censorship. . . . Even if you can't get penalized, you self-censor yourself, you say, "No no no, this is untouchable, I'm not going to talk on this [subject]." (Journalist 4, personal communication, May 28, 2016)

In addition to promoting peace, journalists want to right the wrongs of their predecessors during the genocide. One journalist in a management role at another commercial outlet, Great Lakes Voice, that no longer publishes, said, "The civil society, the media, the parties, the politicians—you failed in the genocide. Therefore, here, we don't want you to do the same mistakes" (Journalist 23, personal communication, June 5, 2016).

The ways journalists in Rwanda perceive their roles are consistent with development media theory (McQuail, 1983), which suggests that media freedom should take a back seat to development aims, and helps explain the Western perspective that a lack of watchdog reporting equates to low levels of press freedom. But journalists in Rwanda are less likely to view their collaboration with the government as repressive and more likely to explain that it is necessary to work with the government for the good of the country, which aligns with Hachten and Scotton's (2012) notion of the developmental concept in which journalists promote nation-building by supporting the work of the government. Numerous journalists explained that this is necessary because of Rwanda's history and the role of media in perpetuating the genocide. Of course, it is possible journalists did not speak openly in our interviews; given the restrictions on free speech, they are not allowed to criticize the government, including in their conversations with us. It is also possible, and understandable, that journalists in Rwanda genuinely want to contribute to peacekeeping. The 1994 genocide against the Tutsi directly influenced the evolution of press freedom in the country and demonstrates the importance of considering a society's distance from civil conflict in frameworks examining a nation's media system.

Public Trust in Media Remains High

Perhaps their commitment to promoting unity and reconciliation is one reason journalists in the country are widely trusted by the public. In general, Rwandan citizens trust authority (now and during the time of the genocide against the Tutsi) in a way many individuals living in Western countries do not. Rwanda was, and still is, a highly religious country, and "People are raised and taught to take what they hear on the radio as gospel truth" (Kamilindi, 2007, p. 136). So, in 1994, when the voices on the radio were empowering Hutus and encouraging them to eliminate their Tutsi neighbours, many complied. Considering how the news media, largely run by party hardliners, so maliciously manipulated the public, it is hard to imagine, at least on the surface, how citizens could regain trust in both political and media institutions. And indeed one researcher suggested that journalists believe they are not trusted because of their role in the genocide (Moon, 2021). Yet, other research has revealed the opposite when talking to members of the public: that despite decreasing trust in several Anglo-Saxon countries, trust in media (and in political leadership) remains high in Rwanda almost three decades after the genocide. And Rwandans explained why that is.

Focus groups conducted among members of the general public in Rwanda in 2018 revealed widespread trust in news media, especially state-run media (McIntyre & Sobel Cohen, 2021a). Individuals said they trust government-run news media because of the role political leaders—namely, Kagame—played in ending the genocide. One member of the public said, "Because they [the public] know that they [the government] stopped the genocide, they believe that they can't do the bad things. That's why they trust the public media" (McIntyre & Sobel Cohen, 2021a, p. 818). The majority of citizens involved in the focus groups said they trust state-run media despite acknowledging that such media primarily report stories about progress and avoid critical or negative coverage. Several individuals said public news media have been known to withhold negative information—for example, by downplaying the number of lives lost in a natural disaster—to protect the public. They said public media houses withhold negative information to prevent the public, especially older, less educated citizens who live in rural villages and are still scarred from surviving the civil war, from panicking (McIntyre & Sobel Cohen, 2021a). This type of censorship was largely not perceived as repressive, but rather as necessary—even appreciated—to maintain public safety. Many Rwandans are willing to sacrifice press freedom for safety, supporting McQuail's theory that news media should take a backseat to the political, economic, social and cultural needs of a country in order to promote development (McQuail, 2010). Many citizens said they would prefer their censored state-run media over media that openly criticize and report negative information, as can be seen in the United States (McIntyre & Sobel Cohen, 2021a). The fact that many Rwandans, because of their history, support this type of censorship and think it is imperative to preserve peace highlights the need to contextualize ideas of press freedom.

The high level of public trust in news media might further be explained by the cultural values in the country. In some ways similar to *ubuntu* philosophy, discussed in Chapter 1, it is common for communities across the African continent, including in Rwanda, to be communalistic (Moemeka, 1994), in which "individuals exist first to serve the community and second to benefit themselves through such communal service" (Moemeka, 1997, p. 174). In communalistic societies, individuals hold a deep respect for authority in all its forms (formal and informal authority figures), and are expected to contribute positively to society in whatever ways authorities direct them. Further, many African nations have high "in-group collectivism" scores, which measure the extent to which a person "expresses pride, loyalty, and cohesiveness in their organizations, families, or circle of close friends" (Chhokar et al., 2008, p. 3). High in-group collectivism "will cause followers to resist challenging leadership, therefore creating followers with less critical thinking" (Thomas, 2014, p. 127). Presumably, this value of personal responsibility to obey authority and protect the community contributed to Rwandans' ability to carry out a genocide, but has also enabled the country to heal and move forward post-genocide. As mentioned in Chapter 1, as part of the nation's reconciliation efforts, a system of justice called gacaca courts was established. In this restorative justice system, "essentially local village councils [exist] where people confess and are punished but are mostly forgiven and reintegrated into the communities from which they came" (Zakaria, 2009, p. 7). Perpetrators and victims' family members now live side by side in villages around the country. These communalistic and ubuntu-based cultural ideals likely also contribute to journalists' acceptance of self-censorship, which might be amplified in this post-genocide time, when Rwandans are undivided in their shared goal not to repeat the past.

Social and Economic Progress Proves Unprecedented

The remainder of this chapter explains how Rwanda has seen substantial progress in recent decades and has, since the genocide against the Tutsi, obtained steady gains in democracy and press freedom, but some indicators suggest that this trend is not likely to continue.

By numerous measures, expanding far beyond high public trust in the media, Rwanda's unification efforts appear to be working. We see this through rapid progress in the country, including in the media sector and beyond. As mentioned in Chapter 1, the number of media houses—public and private—has skyrocketed, and journalism is a field of study at the University of Rwanda and other post-secondary schools such as the Catholic Institute of Kabgayi. The Constitution guarantees freedom of the press, and although journalists are not free to criticize the president, they do perceive their freedoms to be increasing. Developments in the media sector are occurring alongside progress in other areas, economic, social, and technological.

Rwanda has experienced notable economic growth in recent years, averaging 7.5% growth from 2008 to 2018 and per capita gross domestic product (GDP) growth at 5% per year (World Bank, 2020a). Almost all of this growth is attributed to public investments. The Ministry of Finance (2017) has undertaken multiple economic development plans, including an ambitious seven-year plan (2017–2024) called the National Strategy for Transformation in which the Rwandan government aspires to reach Middle-Income Country status by 2035 and High-Income Country status by 2050 via sustained economic growth. This economic development has come alongside staggering progress in education, health care, and social equality. Rwanda has seen reductions in poverty levels (The World Bank, 2020a)—although the data has been contested (Wilson & Blood, 2019)—and increasing literacy rates (Nyirimanzi, 2014). The literacy rate was approximately 73% as of 2018, though it remained lower among women than men (UNESCO, 2018). The nation can be credited with some of the highest elementary school enrollment rates in the continent, although rates in secondary school and universities remain lower (The World Bank, 2020b). Rwanda has a higher percentage of females in parliament than any other country (Buchholz, 2022). And life expectancy has more than doubled since the genocide against the Tutsi (The World Bank, 2020c).

In conjunction with the economic initiatives, in 2000, the Rwandan Ministry of Finance and Economic Planning revealed Rwanda Vision 2020, the nation's ambitious plan to, among other goals, become a "knowledge-based economy" that will "actively encourage science and technology education and ICT skills" (Rwanda Vision 2020, 2000, p. 4). As of the end of 2021, an estimated 45.1% of Rwandans had access to the internet (Internet World Stats, 2022). Compared to neighbours in the region that have experienced civil conflict—Uganda at 39.3%, Burundi at 12.8%, and Democratic Republic of Congo at 17.4%—Rwanda's internet penetration is high (Internet World Stats, 2022). President Kagame publicly encourages his citizens to adopt new technologies and create tech-focused innovations (Collins, 2013; Kagame, 2019a). He has championed the accessibility of smartphones, saying on Twitter, "Smartphones should not be a luxury item. Let's challenge ourselves to make Smartphones an everyday tool enabling all Rwandans to fulfill their potential" (Kagame, 2019b). Rwanda has the second-fastest-growing mobile phone market in East Africa behind Kenya (Okeleke & Pedros, 2018). And Kagame has brokered deals to bring the headquarters and factories of tech companies to Rwanda, including what has been referred to as "Africa's 'first high tech smartphone factory'" (Monks, 2019, para. 1).

Overall, Rwanda has made impressive social, economic, and technological progress since the 1994 genocide against the Tutsi, steadily increasing its development, democratization, and media freedoms. But it remains a nation with tension as its progress at times appears unaligned with its tight government control (Lang, 2018), including what many perceive as wide-reaching limitations on free speech maintained by an oppressive ruler.

President Kagame Maintains Tight Reins

Rwanda has undoubtedly made substantial progress since 1994, but that progress has come at the hands of a single leader, Paul Kagame, who has since been at the forefront of Rwandan politics since he commanded the rebel army (the RPF) that ended the genocide against the Tutsi. Kagame is a complicated figure. He has been referred to as a "darling tyrant" because "he is a dictator responsible for human rights abuses but . . . despite this, he has a great many friends," including leaders of many Western nations (Sundaram, 2014, para. 1). Western media and NGOs consistently publish stories and reports attempting to explain how President Kagame has so effectively maintained almost complete control over his country, including the media sector, while simultaneously receiving admiration from foreign leaders. Former U.S. President Bill Clinton and former United Kingdom Prime Minister Tony Blair lauded the country's progress under Kagame, and Clinton referred to Kagame as "one of the greatest leaders of our time" (Smith, 2012). At the same time, reputable U.S. and European sources have referred to Kagame as a dictator in disguise, a despot in disguise, and a benevolent dictator (Berman, 2016; Cascais, 2020; Flanagan, 2018). Associated Press Uganda correspondent Rodney Muhumuza (2020) points to the seemingly contradictory attitudes toward President Kagame, stating how the leader is both praised and feared, "feted by those who say [Rwanda] needs his visionary leadership and loathed by others who see a firm authoritarian with a malicious streak" (para. 1).

Kagame takes issue with outsiders who criticize him or the country for existing problems instead of focusing on how far it has come. "[Kagame's] attitude is: You're telling me? . . . In his view, the West is in no position to scold Rwanda, where the legacy of colonialism led directly to the genocide" (Gourevitch, 2009, para. 5). Kagame's reelection in August 2017, which he won with 99% of the vote, was made possible by a constitutional amendment that allowed him to run for a third term and remain in office until 2034 (McVeigh, 2015). Many outsiders considered this to be a rigged election, or "more of a coronation than real contest" (Reyntjens, 2017, para. 1). Ongoing human rights abuses continue to be documented in the country, including severe and widespread political repression: "After years of threats, intimidation, mysterious deaths, and high profile, politically motivated trials, few opposition parties remain active or make public comments on government policies" (Human Rights Watch, 2020, para. 3). Most voices of opposition come from outside the country, either from Rwandans in exile or from members of the international community. As a result, scholars and activists have suggested varying points in which Rwanda sits on a spectrum of authoritarianism.

Even maintaining peace comes as a government mandate in Rwanda. In 1999, the RPF initiated a program of national unity and reconciliation, "an ambitious top-down social reengineering project designed to forge a unified Rwandan identity while fostering reconciliation between Tutsi survivors of the genocide and its Hutu perpetrators" (Thomson, 2014, p. 2). This effort resulted in a National Unity and Reconciliation Commission established by law that, among other tasks, creates programs to promote national unity (National Unity and Reconciliation Commission, 2020). Commissioners appointed by President Kagame, along with other staff, make monthly visits to the countryside to monitor such efforts, as participating in unification activities is "a non-negotiable option for Rwandese" (Thomson, 2013, p. 119).

While the Rwandan public largely goes along with the government's unification efforts, it is unclear to what extent that is because they fear the consequences of dissent or because they genuinely share the same goals. Likely, the truth is somewhere in the middle. It stands to reason that individuals who were impacted by genocide want to avoid such conflict in the future, which helps explain why Rwandan citizens, journalists, and non-journalists alike cooperate in peacekeeping efforts; at the same time, Rwandans are the products of a highly effective, decades-long public relations campaign that trained them not to speak out or create conflict. Perhaps the government's strict control over its citizens has been especially effective because of the country's traditional cultural values. As mentioned, Rwanda can be understood as a communalistic society with high "in-group collectivism" where individuals prioritize community over individual success and highly value respect for authority (Chhokar et al., 2008; Moemeka, 1994). These values likely help President Kagame maintain tight control.

And indeed, government criticism is rare. President Kagame has responded to criticism of running an authoritarian regime by saying the public is overwhelmingly supportive of the country's political system. He fails to mention that supporting him and his government is essentially required; for example, local officials are ordered to ensure a strong turnout at Kagame's campaign rallies and other events, at least according to Fred Muvunyi, a former chairman of the Rwanda Media Commission who was pressured to resign from that position and sought political asylum in Germany (Muvunyi, 2017).[2] Those who have spoken out as political opponents have been jailed, forced into exile, or have died mysteriously (Arieff, 2019). Those who attend opponents' rallies (which are rare, as the government limits political opponents from acting freely or criticizing government practices) are watched, as it is common for the government to conduct surveillance on individuals who might be a threat (Arieff, 2019; Human Rights Watch, 2018; Muvunyi, 2017). And *umudugudu* chiefs, or community leaders, are tasked with monitoring the activities of all individuals in their villages. This level of surveillance might have contributed to a submissive, fearful public. In sum, " 'years of state intimidation and interference' have weakened the capacity of local civil society or media outlets to act as a check on state power" (Arieff, 2019, p. 4). And a repressed civil society makes it a challenge for a democratic press to flourish, further helping to explain the state of press freedom in the country. President Kagame's tight control over civil society, resulting from the genocide against the Tutsi, might have helped the country maintain an upward trajectory of development in the years following the civil war, but its long-term impact is yet to be determined.

Future of Press Freedom Remains Uncertain

Will Rwanda's steady gains toward more democratic values, including free speech, continue? There are reasons to believe this linear path of progress may not continue. Despite countless positive achievements in recent decades, Rwanda faces democratic challenges related to political participation, judicial independence, and checks on government, leading it to be labeled a non-democracy (International Institute for Democracy and Electoral Assistance, 2019). Matfess (2015) suggested that Rwanda is an example of developmental authoritarianism, described as "nominally democratic governments that provide significant public works and services while exerting control over nearly every facet of society" (p. 181). Rwanda is also said to be one of seven African nations considered an unreformed autocracy in which "governments make no pretense at legitimizing themselves through competitive elections. . . . In these countries, political liberalization either is never attempted or is captured and distorted by faction leaders who stand to gain from the demise of central authority" (Bratton et al., 2005, p. 18). Rayarikar (2017) argued that "Rwanda is developing towards a completely authoritarian state structure" (p. 1). In its 2020 report, the Ibrahim Index of African Governance, a tool that measures and monitors governance performance in African countries, indicates "warning signs" in Rwanda's overall governance and specifically related to its violence against citizens, executive compliance with the rule of law, and accountability and transparency, among other topic areas.

The political science framework of super-presidentialism (Colton & Skach, 2005; van de Walle, 2003) could also be at play, suggesting that Rwanda's rapid development may soon be stunted. The theory of super-presidentialism suggests that "formally and informally unconstrained presidents will often take steps to concentrate executive authority. Institutions that concentrate executive authority erode democratic institutions. Presidents, provided limited institutional constraints, can pursue policies that neutralize their oppositions and consolidate their incumbency" (Lust & Waldner, 2015, p. 13). Super-presidentialism has been linked to weakening electoral freedom and democratic backsliding, which Rakner (2018) and others have suggested is occurring in Rwanda. Democratic backsliding has been defined as "a change in a combination of competitive electoral procedures, civil and political liberties, and accountability," which "occurs through a series of discrete changes in the rules and informal procedures that shape those elections, rights, and accountability" (Lust & Waldner, 2015, p. 2). Democratic backsliding can be difficult to pinpoint because the changes can be subtle and they can take place over months or years, and the changes can also be "seemingly contradictory; for instance, there may be a clampdown on civil liberties at the same time that new elections are called and new parties allowed to participate" (Lust & Waldner, 2015, p. 10).

Voltmer (2013) argues:

> Almost two decades after the genocide many observers still regard the situation in Rwanda as being volatile, with hatred looming under the surface, which arguably justifies the restrictions that have been imposed on public speech (Kinzer, 2010). However, it becomes increasingly apparent that restrictions on free speech in the name of interethnic peace serve as a smokescreen for endemic censorship. While it is questionable whether the cloak of silence that lies over the society helps to overcome the traumas of the past, it certainly helps to stabilize the power positions of those who are in charge of the transition. (pp. 192–193)

With regard to the nation's intense censorship, including the wide-reaching laws on divisionism and genocide ideology, Voltmer has this to say:

> If difficult truths are swept under the carpet, they are still there and everybody in the room knows it. At some point a society that is struggling with a violent past has to address these issues, otherwise there is the risk that continuing silence will generate new hostilities, conspiracy theories and mistrust among citizens. The solution, however, is not unrestrained expression of opinions regardless of their consequences. . . . press freedom cannot be absolute even in the most robust democracies. Rather, the principle of free speech encompasses both the freedom and dignity of the speaker and the listener. What post-conflict societies therefore need is an open debate about possible limitations of what can be said in the public domain and how this can be justified. (Voltmer, 2013, pp. 193–194)

Taken together, these political ideologies and perspectives may indicate that Rwanda is in a state of "productive liminality"—when a nation is "suspended (potentially indefinitely) in a status 'betwixt and between' mass violence, authoritarianism, and democracy" (Beresford et al., 2018, p. 1231). While we cannot definitively state which of these titles most accurately applies to Rwanda today, it is clear that Kagame operates a form of authoritarianism alongside positive development achievements, making it evident that despite the long list of positive accomplishments, the nation is not necessarily on a linear path toward democratization, and thus increasing media freedoms.

As it relates to press freedom · and media development, present-day Rwanda can be seen as a representation of McQuail's (1983) development media theory, which asserts that "the media are required to join the government in the task of nation building" (p. 188), and Hachten's (1981) developmental concept. This system appears to have worked, at least as it relates to short-term development. When journalists avoid identifying individuals' ethnicities, they promote stability in society. When journalists report on the positive achievements of the government instead of, say, corruption, they help to strengthen morale. When journalists view their role, at least in part, as unifiers, they promote the maintenance of peace. Given the relatively recent genocide against the Tutsi, these actions of journalists are contributing to the immediate reconstruction and nation-building that is taking place in the country. The efforts of the journalists, taken in conjunction with the work of the government, appear to be helping the country achieve short-term economic, social, and infrastructure progress.

However, we, and other critics, argue that now, nearly 30 years after the genocide against the Tutsi, by conforming to the desires of the government, journalists are doing the opposite of promoting development—instead, they are hindering it. While it could be argued that short-term development can lead to long-term development, primarily via peace and stability, concerns have been raised about the long-term ramifications of widespread self-censorship, such as journalists losing their credibility, but most notably their inability to hold power to account, thus threatening the future of the profession (Yesil, 2014). Self-censorship and the inability to hold power to account in Rwanda may, in the long term, reinforce the existing social and political structure and restricted press freedom landscape.

It is clear that the relatively recent genocide in the country directly and powerfully impacted media freedoms through resulting laws, policies, leadership, and professional and cultural norms. These examples lend support to Musa's (1997) call for a "practicable media theory for development" that takes into account "the historical contexts that gave rise to the present media systems" (p. 143). We agree that the historical context of a country must be considered when understanding its level of press freedom, but we argue that precisely because the context of each country is unique, no one theory for media development will apply to all countries all the time. Distance from civil conflict is one element to examine when studying press freedom and media ecosystems. In Rwanda, we see a relationship between press freedom and distance from conflict, suggesting that the more time that has passed since a country has experienced civil war, the more press freedom it has. On the surface, this relationship seems to hold when looking at other countries in the region, as well; Kenya has maintained relative peace and, thus, undeniably more press freedom than Rwanda, for example. But when you dive deeper into the mediascapes of countries during and after social conflict, the relationship becomes less clear. We are seeing signs that Rwanda's linear path toward increasing democracy and press freedom may not continue, and as Uganda has moved further away from conflict, some media restrictions have lessened and others have worsened. And even when this press freedom and distance from conflict relationship holds true, it is not enough to be a singular measure of press freedom, as it certainly is not always linear. The realities of other factors, most notably political fluctuations, can and do cause democratic backsliding and setbacks in media freedoms. Such has been the case in Uganda and Kenya, the focus of the next two chapters.

Notes

1. Although unrelated, it should also be noted that the journalists highly valued their role to provide entertainment (McIntyre & Sobel Cohen, 2022).
2. An opinion article in *The New Times* accused Muvunyi of acting unethically and loaning out his name for others to use as a byline to gain credibility when criticizing the president (Karemera, 2019).

3

Uganda

Ebbs and Flows in Press Freedom and Democracy in the Pearl of Africa

Much of Africa has experienced rapid development in recent decades, and with such development has come increasing demands for democratic governance (Mukhongo, 2010). Specifically in sub-Saharan Africa, countries "have made notable, across-the-board progress towards sustainable and comprehensive democracy" (Mukhongo, 2010, p. 342). Since "media freedom is a necessary condition for democratization" (Becker et al., 2007, p. 5), we continue our discussion in this chapter by thoroughly examining the state of press freedom from varying perspectives in Uganda and what influences have hindered and facilitated such freedoms over time. In Chapter 2, we demonstrated how Rwanda has appeared to show a generally steady increase in press freedom since the 1994 genocide against the Tutsi, but we explained how this upward trajectory may not continue. In the next two chapters, we show how the road to media freedom has been bumpier in Uganda and Kenya, countries that are further removed from civil conflict. This chapter shows how press freedom and democratization are not linear and reinforces that each nation's contextual factors must be considered when evaluating press freedom.

Perceptions of Press Freedom

Outsiders' Perspective

Perceptions of press freedom in Uganda are deceiving. On one hand, Uganda's constitution promises freedom of expression (Kimumwe, 2014; Maractho, 2015; Odongo, 2014), the country is said to be one of the most free and active media landscapes in Central and East Africa, and courts have ruled in favor of journalists' rights (Freedom House, 2022b), pointing to a

Press Freedom and the (Crooked) Path Toward Democracy. Meghan Sobel Cohen and Karen McIntyre Hopkinson,
Oxford University Press. © Oxford University Press 2023. DOI: 10.1093/oso/9780197634202.003.0003

recipe for a free and vibrant media ecosystem. At the same time, the nation has had the same leader, President Yoweri Museveni, since 1986, who is regularly referred to as a dictator (Akumu, 2014; Simon, 2019) and has a "conflict-ridden history" with spurts of severe political violence (Matovu & Stewart, 2000, p. 240). Further, journalists report ongoing and sustained efforts to limit free expression (Chibita & Fourie, 2007; Isoba, 1980). The Ugandan government has a long history of suppressing the press (Chibita & Fourie, 2007), and an array of legal and extralegal mechanisms continues to limit free expression. Indicators point to decreasing press freedom in the country in recent years and decades.

In the 2022 Reporters Without Borders World Press Freedom Index, Uganda was rated 132nd out of 180, down seven spots from 2021, down 15 spots from 2018, and down a striking 80 spots since 2002 (Reporters Without Borders, 2022d), indicating a sharp decline in press freedom. This decline is not unique to Uganda. As mentioned in Chapter 1, most people around the world have experienced a decline in their country's freedom of expression in recent years (UNESCO, 2022).

Scholars and activists have described a highly restricted press sector, noting that security officials target journalists and detain them without cause, especially when reporting on opposition activities, and similarly, authorities beat journalists, abduct them, or take away their equipment or journalism license (Namusoke, 2018; Reporters Without Borders, 2022d). A crackdown on journalists was enhanced in 2017, when a team of officials was tasked with monitoring social media posts to search for government criticism. Since then, authorities have raided radio stations and interrupted broadcasts on multiple occasions to stop interviews with an opposition candidate (Reporters Without Borders, 2019b). Freedom House (2017) said the Ugandan government and press have "settled into a predictable relationship" where the government sometimes "lashes out" at the press, but "such heavy-handed actions tend not to permanently disrupt operations" (para. 6). Höglund and Schaffer (2021) described this as "a never-ending sword-play between publishers and the government" (p. 518).

Given these grim facts, on the surface it may be hard to understand why Uganda is credited with being one of the more free and active media landscapes in the region. Here's the explanation: The media sector is thought to be liberalized due to a sharp uptick in the number of media houses in the 1990s. However, more media houses does not equal more media freedom (Sobel Cohen & McIntyre, 2020a). So, while the profession appears liberalized from the outside, journalists remain restricted. As mentioned in Chapter 1, this paradox may be explained in part by the safety valve theory, a political science framework that describes states where citizens are allowed to speak out against the government, and because they are free to do so, they feel as if they have sufficient space to air their grievances and thus, refrain from violent protests (Buehler, 2013). Perhaps a safety valve is occurring in Uganda, a semi-authoritarian state where the appearance of a liberalized media system can blur the line between a free press and a restricted press, and is ultimately reinforcing existing power structures (Sobel Cohen & McIntyre, 2020a). This is consistent with Tripp's (2004) argument that rulers of semi-authoritarian regimes, such as President Museveni, only implement the reforms necessary to appear democratic to international donors. "Not far beneath the rhetorical veneer of democratization one finds actions that undermine existing elements of political liberalization, actions that are sacrificed to keep the dominant party or head of state in power at all costs" (Tripp, 2004, p. 7).

Insiders' Perspective[*]

Unlike in Rwanda, where outsiders perceive low levels of press freedom but journalists in the country feel the opposite, journalists in Uganda largely agree with the international perception that they are restricted, and the situation is worsening. In our 2019 survey, journalists in Uganda were most likely to agree with their press freedom ranking of 125th out of 180 countries (55.6% of respondents agreed with that assessment) compared to journalists in Kenya or Rwanda, who agreed with their ranking at a rate of 40.2% and 29.8%, respectively. While some journalists in Uganda disagreed with the ranking because they felt they had more freedom, the highest percentage (20.3%) disagreed because they felt they had less freedom than the ranking indicated. All three countries' 2019 press freedom rankings can be seen in Table 3.1, and Rwandan and Ugandan journalists' agreement with their rankings can be seen in Figure 3.1.

In the same survey, we asked how journalists in the three nations perceive the level of press freedom in their respective countries, regardless of

---

*Portions of this sub-section are published in McIntyre, K., & Sobel Cohen, M. (2021), Salary, Suppression, and Spies: Journalistic Challenges in Uganda, *Journalism Studies*, 22(2), 243–261; and Sobel Cohen, M., & McIntyre, K. (2020), The State of Press Freedom in Uganda, *International Journal of Communication*, 14, 649–668.

Table 3.1 Reporters Without Borders Press Freedom
Ranking in 2019, the Year Our Survey Was Distributed

Rwanda = 155th out of 179 countries
Uganda = 125th out of 179 countries
Kenya = 100th out of 179 countries

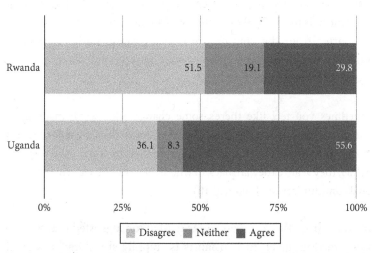

Figure 3.1 Rwandan and Ugandan Journalists' Level of Agreement With Their
2019 Reporters Without Borders Press Freedom Ranking

international rankings. The data show that journalists in Uganda reported
significantly lower levels of perceived press freedom than journalists in the
other two countries. They estimated their level of press freedom to be, on
average, 44.85 on a scale from 1 to 100 with 100 indicating the most freedom
(significantly less freedom than they said they would prefer to have, 92.93).
Journalists in the other two countries estimated their levels of press freedom
to be about 20 points higher on that scale.

Not only did journalists in Uganda perceive their press freedom to
be lower than journalists in their neighbouring countries, they also had a
more pessimistic view of their levels of press freedom in the past and future. Journalists in Uganda estimated their level of press freedom 25 years
ago (from the time the survey was administered) to be nearly equal to their
current level: 42.01 on the same 100-point scale. Journalists in Rwanda and
Kenya perceived their levels of press freedom a quarter-century ago to be

significantly lower than present-day levels. And looking 10 years into the future, Ugandan journalists predicted their level of press freedom would only increase by three points (to 47.55 out of 100). Journalists in Rwanda and Kenya predicted that their levels of press freedom in 10 years' time would increase by 11 points. See Rwandan and Ugandan journalists' perceived level of press freedom over time in Figure 3.2.

In our interviews with journalists in Uganda in 2018, the long-standing ebbs and flows of press freedom were clearly articulated, and the feeling that press freedom is in a period of decline was a major theme.

A reporter from the commercial outlet Uganda Radio Network aptly summarized the "never-ending sword-play between publishers and the government" referenced above:

> Sometimes you feel like there's some change, like, we've made a step. Journalists are able to speak for themselves. Journalists are able to take action against anyone who tries to infringe on their freedom. And then, after a while, they realize they are back to where they started. (Journalist 15, personal communication, June 7, 2018)

An editor from the commercial *Daily Monitor* suggested that the amount of press freedom given to journalists is "rapidly shrinking" (Journalist 1,

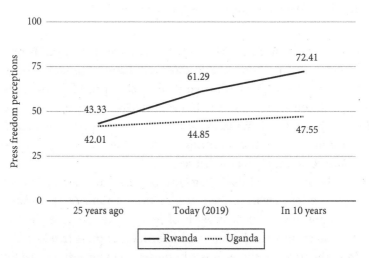

Figure 3.2 Rwandan and Ugandan Journalists' Perceived Level of Press Freedom Over Time
Note. 0 = no freedom; 100 = full freedom.

personal communication, June 4, 2018). Similarly, a reporter from the *Daily Monitor* said, "We have a long way to go" in the fight for free expression (Journalist 6, personal communication, June 5, 2018).

Journalists continued to speak about the factors contributing to this decline. These challenges are discussed next.

Challenges to Press Freedom: Political Actions and Ideologies

Journalists from all three countries—Rwanda, Uganda, and Kenya—ranked a fear of government retaliation and repressive national laws, such as those related to defamation or access to information, as either the most or second-most important factors impacting press freedom in our 2019 survey. (See how journalists in all three countries ranked factors that most influence their press freedom in Table 3.3.) Yet, the specific ways journalists are restricted vary and are the direct result of each country's political history and current administration. Our interview data reveal specific details that put these restrictions in context.

Political History Leaves Impact

Uganda's mediascape has always been, and still is, inextricably tied to the country's political structure. Uganda gained independence from Britain in 1962, and the following years can be understood in four periods: Obote's first period of rule (1962–1971), the Amin era (1971–1979), a transition and then Obote's second period of rule (1980–1985), then a transition and Museveni's rule (1985–present). Documented censorship of the press existed during colonial days as well as since "the country's first post independence head of government, Milton Obote who became prime minister in 1962, banned the intellectual Rajat Neogy's *Transition* magazine. Idi Amin overthrew Obote in 1971—during his regime, key journalists disappeared without trace. The press was a central target during the second Obote government between 1980–1985 and its military successor" (Ssenoga, 2018, para. 4–5).

After contested elections in 1986, Museveni declared himself president and was subsequently elected to the presidency in 1996, 2001, and 2006 (Oloka-Onyango, 2004). Museveni's early days in office brought promises

Table 3.2 Uganda: Interviewee, Job Title, Employer, and Type of Organization

Participant	Job Title	Employer	Type of Org.
Journalist 1	Editor	Daily Monitor	Commercial
Journalist 2	Former journalist	Human Rights Network for Journalists	NGO
Journalist 3	Reporter	NBS	Commercial
Journalist 4	Reporter	Daily Monitor	Commercial
Journalist 5	Photojournalist	Daily Monitor	Commercial
Journalist 6	Reporter	Daily Monitor	Commercial
Journalist 7	Editor/Reporter	Monitor Publications Ltd.	Commercial
Journalist 8	Management role	CEO Magazine	Commercial
Journalist 9	Journalist	Eagle Online	Commercial
Journalist 10	Senior Reporter	New Vision	Government
Journalist 11	Anchor/Reporter	Urban TV	Gov./Commercial
Journalist 12	Reporter	Name withheld	Government
Journalist 13	Reporter	Agence France-Presse*	Commercial
Journalist 14	Photojournalist	Agence France-Presse*	Commercial
Journalist 15	Reporter	Uganda Radio Network	Commercial
Journalist 16	Journalist	Buganda Broadcasting Service (BBS)	Gov./Commercial
Journalist 17	Reporter	Uganda Radio Network	Commercial
Journalist 18	Former reporter	Uganda Hub for Investigative Media	NGO
Journalist 19	Videographer	BBC*	Gov./Commercial
Journalist 20	Photojournalist	New Vision	Government
Journalist 21	Journalist	Daily Monitor	Commercial
Journalist 22	Journalist	Chimp Reports	Commercial
Journalist 23	Correspondent	Daily Monitor	Commercial
Journalist 24	Reporter	Uganda Radio Network	Commercial
Journalist 25	Reporter	Bukedde TV	Government
Journalist 26	Journalist	NTV	Commercial
Journalist 27	Management role	The East African*	Commercial

* Foreign news outlet (not headquartered in the country where the interview occurred)

Table 3.3 Journalists' Rankings of Seven Factors that Most Influence Their Press Freedom

Rwanda	Uganda	Kenya
Fear of gov't. retaliation (M = 2.36)	Fear of gov't. retaliation (M = 1.95)	National laws (M = 2.04)
National laws (M = 2.81)	National laws (M = 2.45)	Fear of gov't. retaliation (M = 2.86)
Self-censor to not upset owner (M = 3.44)	Self-censor to not upset owner (M = 3.34)	Self-censor to not lose ads (M = 3.16)
Self-censor to not lose ads (M = 3.78)	Self-censor to not lose ads (M = 3.86)	Self-censor to not upset owner (M = 3.28)
Fear of retaliation from journalists (M = 4.31)	Fear of retaliation from journalists (M = 4.71)	Self-censor to protect citizens/promote peace (M = 4.80)
Self-censor to protect citizens/promote peace (M = 4.54)	Self-censor to protect citizens/promote peace (M = 5.02)	Fear of retaliation from journalists (M = 4.89)
Other (M = 6.76)	Other (M = 6.66)	Other (M = 6.96)

and hope of change, but by the mid-1990s things had taken a turn for the worse again, with "the government shutting down media platforms, legal threats, the infiltration of newsrooms by security spies, thuggery, intimidation and withholding of advertising from institutions deemed to be critical of the government" (Ssenoga, 2018, para. 13).

Museveni remains president today and has made notable social and economic developments during his time in office, including a fight against the Lord's Resistance Army (LRA); but Museveni and his ruling party, the National Resistance Movement (NRM) (and its military wing, the National Resistance Army), have been involved in multiple civil conflicts beginning in the 1980s and continuing into the early 2000s.

Museveni and his NRM government operate a semi-authoritarian or hybrid regime (Fisher & Anderson, 2015; Tangri & Mwenda, 2008; Tripp, 2004). As of 1995, Uganda has had a multi-party system and a democratic constitution that guarantees freedom of expression and freedom of the press, yet whenever the NRM feels threatened, it clamps down on dissenting voices for the purpose of staying in power. Government has shrunk the democratic space and twice changed the constitution to allow Museveni to continue to run for president, removing a two-term limit in 2005 and a 75-year presidential age limit in 2017.

The complexities of Ugandan history and the particularities of the conflicts are beyond the scope of this summary, but they led to devastating civil unrest, particularly in the northern region: a "bush war" in the 1980s, multiple rebellions and insurgencies, and a decades-long insurgency of the LRA, led by Joseph Kony, which resulted in widespread death and destruction, the abduction of children for the use of child soldiers and sex slaves, and an estimated 1.5 to 1.9 million internally displaced persons (Human Rights Watch, 2012; International Crisis Group, 2004). Massacres conducted at the hands of the LRA led to criticism about Museveni's ability to defend citizens and defeat the insurgency.

Throughout the conflict with the LRA in the northern part of the country, journalists who reported on crimes committed by the Ugandan army were labeled rebel supporters (Human Rights Watch, 2010), which is consistent with previous research suggesting a longstanding culture of secrecy and lack of press freedom surrounding the Ugandan army (Onadipe & Lord, 1999; Wolfsfeld, 1997). Additionally, Ugandan officials restricted reporters' access to certain regions of the country (Committee to Protect Journalists, 2007), and journalists who reported on the conflict with the LRA in Northern Uganda were found to have faced "warning, arrest, harassment, assault, court proceedings and imprisonment by the government—due to the publication of information that is deemed to be contrary to the government's view" (Acayo & Mnjama, 2004, para. 35).

A reporter for the *Daily Monitor* also explained that much of the coverage about wars, including the conflict with the LRA, is tightly controlled and, thus, only shows one perspective—that of the government:

Our stories told by victors are told from a victors' viewpoint. For example, we had five years between 1981 and 1985, a blood war in what is called the Luwero Triangle, the war that brought this regime to power, and the story of that war is largely told from the viewpoint of the current administration. . . . they committed atrocities, they massacred people, they are accused of very serious human rights violations. And now, they circulate a documentary by one of the president's daughters that retells the story of what they call a "liberation struggle" from the viewpoint of the current government that is certainly blind to atrocities that they are accused of committing during the war. [Regarding the conflict with the LRA in Northern Uganda], many of those stories will be told from the viewpoint of [Joseph] Kony, the villain. Yes, he's a villain. He should be crucified tomorrow, but the war certainly had more villains than just Joseph Kony. . . . Many of the men and women in uniform under the current administration . . . should possibly as well be answering questions about gross human rights violations that went beyond the ordinary call of duty in terms of how they responded to attack. So you have gross human rights violations that are committed by the current administration in the course of their war. And that story never gets told. (Journalist 4, personal communication, June 5, 2018)

Recent years have brought peace to Uganda as the LRA withdrew from the country in 2005 and 2006 (though the group is thought to have carried out attacks in recent years in the Democratic Republic of Congo, South Sudan, and the Central African Republic) (United Nations Security Council, 2016). As the conflict with the LRA lessened, some of these restrictions have, too, but Museveni is believed to have used the conflict with the LRA as a means to justify the status quo in Ugandan politics, including his unreformed army, a lack of space for dissent or opposition power, and a crackdown on free expression.

The political history and culture in Uganda has resulted in a certain ideology. "The feeling is that Ugandans owe the Museveni government everything because its leaders sacrificed, shed blood and lost comrades to 'liberate' Uganda" (Tabaire, 2007, p. 208). Therefore, any action that could be perceived as being anti-government is received as a threat. This helps explain why journalists have a hard time getting access to information and why laws are, at times, used to restrict journalists rather than protect them. It also explains why journalists—in our interviews and beyond—complain of inadequate training which can lead to mistakes with unintended consequences: "A simple newspaper mistake is perceived in government circles as conscious misinformation 'by an organized opponent. Criticism is then equated to an act of hostility by an opposition bent on bringing the government down'" (Tabaire, 2007, p. 206). This ideology—that journalists are the opposition—is a direct result of Uganda's political history, and it is easily reinforced as long as the country's leadership remains unchanged. It is wholly undemocratic, and journalists will continue to face increasing repression until the political leadership changes their mindset, or, more likely, changes hands.

Government Interference Still Pervasive

Given its history, it is unsurprising that in Uganda, journalists from our survey cited government retaliation as their biggest hindrance to press freedom. The journalists we interviewed spoke directly to the daily threats and worse, explained above by Reporters Without Borders (2019b, 2022d). One former journalist who now works at the non-profit Human Rights Network for Journalists in Kampala talked about the "loose, underhand method of intimidating the owners, the editors," threatening them not to publish critical stories or they will have their operating licenses revoked (Journalist 2, personal communication, June 4, 2018). Reporters live in fear. They discussed how police officers have intimidated them while driving, passing them dangerously while yelling threats, and how police fail to act when a reporter's laptop is stolen. They also discussed how sometimes the broadcasting signal of a radio or TV station will be cut off when a political opponent is scheduled to speak.

Reporters are especially nervous after they publish a story that targets "the people at the heart of government, which is the president, his family and corrupt ministers," said a reporter from the commercial television network NBS (Journalist 3, personal communication, June 4, 2018). An editor/reporter from Monitor Publications Ltd., which publishes the *Daily Monitor* as well as several other outlets, said, "If you're so critical, you can't be assured of being safe the next days after the story has come out" (Journalist 7, personal communication, June 5, 2018). At the time of our interview, one senior reporter for *New Vision*, the main government-funded media house, said they were still recovering from recently being detained after writing a story about a suspicious death in which they had more information than police:

> I was picked [arrested and/or detained] recently for a story I did. It was a factual story, but of course the issue is that, where did I get the information from? And being a government paper, why did we publish it the way we published the story? . . . They picked me from office here, took me and kept me somewhere for one week. And they all feel it was—So that's the challenge you'll first see. You cannot pass a story without getting that kind of intimidation. (Journalist 10, personal communication, June 6, 2018)

One thing that makes government interference in Uganda so insidious is its precarious nature. The line is not always clear about what information is off limits, and retaliation is inconsistent. A reporter from Uganda Radio Network, an independent Kampala-based news agency, said:

> It's very difficult because, for me, I've worked as a reporter and I've worked as editor, and I've worked both in the government publication and the

private media houses. And in both the private media houses and the government media houses, there's always that invisible hand . . . [it's an] invisible line, really, and you just never know when you've actually crossed it, you know? It's quite difficult. It's scary at times. (Journalist 17, personal communication, June 7, 2018)

Similarly, the reporter from the private TV station NBS said:

There are times when we've had critical stories. We've run them and nothing has been said. You expect some backlash, nothing happens. . . . But then, [there are] other stories where the state is increasingly involved . . . and saying, "You can't run this story."
(Journalist 3, personal communication, June 4, 2018)

Overall, journalists blamed their repressive state on President Museveni, and multiple journalists associated recent declines in press freedom with the length of his rule. For example, the previously quoted reporter from Uganda Radio Network said:

When the current government, the current president Yoweri Museveni, took over our government 31 years ago, he made several promises of press freedom, of access to information. And at the beginning, it was liberal. There was a bit of press freedom. . . . But then, the longer the government stays in power, the worse it gets. (Journalist 17, personal communication, June 7, 2018)

Similarly, a reporter from the *Daily Monitor* said:

I think the [press freedom] space is reducing. It's shrinking. . . . There's no scientific discovery one has to do about that. It's expected. It's a trend that is common with regimes that have overstayed their welcome, whether it's in Africa, whether it's in Vietnam, whether it's in Asia, whether it's in— literally, any corner in the world. . . . [President Museveni has] maintained himself in power for now 32 years, and unless you have a black swan or what, you know, we call "an act of God," you may most likely have him again as president for—his current term will possibly expire in 2021. He has just amended the constitution to remove the age limit. And that means in 2021, again, he will . . . rig himself back into power for another seven years. So, he could easily do 40 years. He's almost unstoppable. . . . Now, what that means is, for you to be able to do that, for a system to achieve that, you achieve that with incredible losses to institutions. (Journalist 4, personal communication, June 5, 2018)

Indeed, Museveni was reelected in 2021 with a reported 58.6% of the votes. Leading up to the election, civil society groups, an African election monitoring group, and foreign governments including the U.S. and U.K. questioned its credibility and transparency, after the Ugandan government shut down the internet the day before the vote and requests for accreditation to monitor the election were denied, among other suspicious activity (Reuters, 2021).

Repressive Laws Restrain Reporters

The 1995 constitution guarantees freedom of expression, but legal mechanisms continue to restrict journalists (Kimumwe, 2014; Maractho, 2015; Odongo, 2014). Simply, laws are hijacked and used to gag the media.

Reporters and editors are charged with libel, sedition, treason, defamation, and other vaguely-written laws whenever they become too critical of the ruling party (Freedom House, 2022b; Kalyango & Eckler, 2010; Mwesige, 2004). For example, some editors have been charged under the Computer Misuse Act, which was intended to maintain a safe environment for electronic transactions but because of vague and confusing language infringes on journalists' (and others') rights to access to information and freedom of expression, according to the Human Rights Network for Journalists in Uganda (2014). "This one seeks to colonize everything I do using my cell phones, my laptop, my computer," said one former journalist who transitioned into working for the Human Rights Network for Journalists (Journalist 2, personal communication, June 4, 2018). That former journalist also spoke about the Anti-Homosexuality Act, which prevents journalists from publishing stories about the topic for fear of being charged with promoting the act of homosexuality. The Uganda Communications Act is also used to restrict journalists. It was intended to develop a modern communications sector, but journalists said it gives too much power to the Uganda Communications Commission, the industry's government-owned but independently run regulatory body. The former journalist said the UCC is constantly threatening to revoke the operating licenses of media houses:

Most media houses here do not have permanent or official licenses for their media houses, even though that they have fulfilled the requirements, are only issued out with provisional licenses, so that in case they see you as trying to "misbehave," you're reminded that you also don't have a substantive license. All you have is a provisional license, which can be withdrawn any time. So, you see, now, using the legal frameworks, it will take back what is already provided for in the constitution. (Journalist 2, personal communication, June 4, 2018)

It is worth noting, however, that according to journalists that we interviewed, although licenses are technically required the rule is not always enforced, and journalists regularly practice without licenses.

Further, many journalists have been charged with defamation:

Majority of those ones have been trying to expose the corrupt government officials, consistently write about them, and how they have misused public funds. Many of such media houses or journalists have been dragged to courts of law. And the state has prosecuted them. So, while you're supposed to play a watchdog role on the government, your work is criminalized, not because you're unfactual but because they think that you are crossing the line. And that becomes a crime for you, especially through using the existing legal frameworks like the law on defamation, which was recently challenged in the East African Court of Justice because it's being used by the powerful government officials to circumvent themselves from public scrutiny and holding them to account. (Journalist 2, personal communication, June 4, 2018)

Other ways the Ugandan government has tried to control speech have been through taxing people to use the internet. In 2018, the country instituted its Over-The-Top tax, which became known as the social media tax. This law required citizens to pay a fee of 200 Ugandan Shillings (about 5 cents) a day to access more than 50 platforms, including popular social media sites like Facebook, Twitter, and WhatsApp. President Museveni initiated the tax to curb gossip on social media and to raise money (Nyeko, 2018). The tax was ineffective; citizens avoided it by using virtual private networks (VPNs). So, in 2021, it was replaced by a new tax on data packages (Mwesigwa, 2021). This tax stifles free speech for journalists and all citizens, and as Mwesigwa (2021) points out, it is in direct opposition to

Uganda's supposed mission to make the internet more inclusive—a mission supported by a $200 million loan from the World Bank in June 2021 (World Bank, 2021).

Journalists in Uganda are further restricted even when laws are in place intended to protect them. For example, the Press and Journalist Act, which proponents said would increase the level of professionalism in the industry, requires journalists to obtain a certificate to practice journalism from the Minister of Information, something that Anite and Nkuubi (2014) said is "against the national, regional and international protocols on freedom of expression" (p. 29). Additionally, government regulations of the press are unevenly upheld (Odongo, 2014), as many owners of commercial media houses have political and financial ties to government officials and, thus, are not held to the same standards and/or take it upon themselves to self-censor and ensure that their journalists are not overly critical of the government (Chibita, 2009).

Despite the legal challenges discussed, it is worth noting that journalists in Uganda have experienced some legal wins. The Human Rights Network for Journalists–Uganda is fully dedicated to fighting for media freedom in the country, and some human rights organizations, independent media houses, and social media celebrities have rallied for the cause. Höglund and Schaffer (2021) describe how journalists have at times been able to push back against state repression and advance the institutional framework for media freedom. They find these efforts to be most successful when the media actors show solidarity, when the issue gains international media attention and public support, when the media house in question is reputable, and when business-as-usual is disrupted and journalists are empowered.

But more often, laws are used to silence journalists. One particularly problematic law is the country's Access to Information Act. This act should allow reporters to obtain documents for their investigations. However, the journalists we interviewed named access to information as one of their biggest challenges. The difficulties are due in part to a lack of knowledge among both journalists and officials. Many journalists do not follow the proper procedures to obtain information through the Access to Information Act, namely, filling out the forms to request specific information, said a former reporter who works with the Uganda Hub for Investigative Media (Journalist 18, personal communication, June 7, 2018). This is due to a lack of knowledge that the forms exist or a lack of skills necessary to complete them, this former reporter said. Journalists also often do not understand the chain of command in certain organizations or institutions, and they seek interviews from those who are not authorized to talk to the media. These issues reflect another challenge, that being inadequate education and professional training. However, journalists are not solely to blame, as some officials do not understand their responsibility to provide such information when it is properly requested (Journalist 18, personal communication, June 7, 2018).

Still, when reporters (and officials) are aware of the proper procedures, the information is not always provided, and this is true across the spectrum, journalists said, including a reporter from the commercial news agency Uganda Radio Network:

> It's government. It's NGOs. It's private businesses. It's just general access to information. People want what they want out. They don't mind what a journalist wants. And actually, when you go out to ask for information, they kind of feel you are looking for something. (Journalist 15, personal communication, June 7, 2018)

Officials are especially tight-lipped when it comes to government institutions. A journalist for the commercial TV station Buganda Broadcasting Service (BBS) said, "The right to access information is not really open here when it comes to government institutions" (Journalist 16, personal communication, June 7, 2018). A correspondent for the *Daily Monitor* agreed: "We are not forward. The government is not willing" (Journalist 23, personal communication, June 11, 2018). The challenge for journalists, and especially for investigative or political reporters, is that the state views them as unpatriotic when they are trying to obtain information. A reporter for a government-run news outlet who asked us to withhold the name of their outlet said, "Sourcing information from them [police and security officials] becomes a problem. Once you tend to have asked questions, you want to get documents, they look at you as a threat" (Journalist 12, personal communication, June 6, 2018). This mentality is a product of Uganda's history.

Unethical Behaviour Creates Vicious Cycle

Worn down by government intimidation and repressive laws, some journalists become discouraged and even desperate. They are further demoralized by their pitiful pay. At the time of our interviews, journalists reported earning between 5,000 and 50,000 Ugandan shillings—approximately 1 to 13 USD—per story, depending on the length of the story and the resources of the media house. They said with such low pay, reporters cannot afford to buy equipment needed in the field. They feel inadequate. More importantly, low pay impacts the integrity of the news coverage. Journalists who are paid per story shy away from sensitive stories in order to ensure their work will be published and they will be compensated. Further, reporters who are poorly paid are more likely to accept bribes. One reporter we interviewed said some media houses intentionally underpay journalists because they count on the fact that their reporters are making extra money in the field through bribes from sources. The acceptance of payment to withhold information or convey an issue or person positively—(brown) envelope journalism, as it has been called (Ndhlovu, 2022)—is said to be "wide- spread in sub-Saharan Africa" (Fiedler & Frère, 2018, p. 130) and has been documented in Ethiopia (Lodamo & Skjerdal, 2009), Cameroon (Ndangam, 2009), and Benin (Adjovi, 2003), among others. In Uganda, at its most mild, a journalist might accept a few shillings from a source involved in a scandal to withhold some embarrassing information. At its most egregious, journalists are regularly and secretly paid by government officials to act as spies.

In fact, the journalists we interviewed said there is a spy in nearly every newsroom in the country. These individuals are recruited by government officials, sometimes against their will. They will tip off officials when their media house is getting ready to publish a sensitive story, which often results in a call to an editor threatening them to kill the story. Or, "sometimes, we even tip them off about, 'Hey, there is a story coming out. I think you could sue these guys for defamation or something.' And you just make sure you have a cut from it," said an anchor/reporter at Urban TV, a station funded by both the government and private individuals (Journalist 11, personal communication, June 6, 2018). A reporter at the *Daily Monitor* said it feels as far-fetched as a movie scene (Journalist 4, personal communication, June 5, 2018). As a result of this deception, reporters told us they do not trust their colleagues. They usually suspect who the spies are and avoid talking to them about the stories they are working on. Some reporters said they always work alone, they keep notes and documents at a friend's house, or they ask to write critical stories in a trusted editor's office.

Journalists blamed the government, lack of press freedom, and poor pay for putting them in this situation, where they feel like they need to compromise their ethics to provide for their families. But they also blamed themselves. "There's a restrictive regime in Uganda but at times, it comes from us," a Ugandan reporter for Agence France-Presse said (Journalist 13, personal communication, June 7, 2018). Similarly, the previously quoted anchor/reporter for Urban TV explained, "We have abused the freedom that we have as journalists, and we've worked in the pockets of politicians" (Journalist 11, personal communication, June 6, 2018). A journalist at the commercial online magazine Eagle Online agreed: "Journalists are some-times the biggest threat to press freedom" (Journalist 9, personal communi-cation, June 6, 2018). In part, they aren't committed to upholding journalistic ethics because they were inadequately trained and not passionate about the industry to begin with, our interviewees said. "The sad bit about it is that I ended up in the newsroom because I didn't pass my high school enough, not because I dreamt of being a journalist as a kid," said the anchor/reporter from Urban TV (Journalist 11, personal communication, June 6, 2018). Further, those who are passionate about the profession—the best journalists—are promoted to editor positions, taking them out of the field. It's easy to see how these factors spiral and create a vicious cycle. Journalists are underpaid, so they supplement their salaries by accepting bribes from corrupt politicians, which they are willing to do because they lack sufficient training, profession-alism, and passion. All this while being the target of government threats and intimidation. No wonder morale is low.

Journalists Pessimistic About Future of Press Freedom

Ugandan journalists were pessimistic—at least the ones we surveyed and interviewed. They repeatedly described press freedom as being in a state of decline in the country, and they were equally pessimistic about their country's path toward democracy. They were significantly less likely than journalists in Rwanda and Kenya to believe their country has a strong de-mocracy. However, survey respondents did not necessarily connect the two topics: they were the least likely to believe the level of press freedom in their country is linked to the strength of democracy in the country. This was sur-prising, especially because Ugandan journalists were more likely to believe the leadership in their country is authoritative than journalists in Rwanda and Kenya, and they ranked government interference—carried out by that authoritarian leadership—as the number one factor affecting press freedom.

See how journalists from each country responded to a series of statements about democracy in Table 3.4.

It may be surprising that Ugandan journalists judged their leadership to be more authoritative than Rwandan journalists, considering Rwanda has a lower press freedom ranking and one might assume that a more authoritative government would allow the least press freedom. These survey results might reflect Rwandan journalists' fear of reporting their true feelings, or they might reflect Ugandan journalists' pessimism in the state of press freedom and democracy in their country. There has been more critical coverage about media suppression in Uganda than Rwanda, which may factor into journalists' thinking. It is worth noting that the Ibrahim Index of African Governance, a tool that measures and monitors governance performance in African countries, ranked Uganda lower than Rwanda in overall governance in its 2020 report (Ibrahim Index of African Governance, 2020).

Ugandan journalists may be pessimistic, but they have grit and self-efficacy. In our survey, they were more likely than Rwandan journalists to believe that journalists in their country have contributed to strengthening democracy (despite being less likely to think that the level of press freedom

Table 3.4 Percentage of Survey Respondents Who Agreed or Strongly Agreed With Select Statements

	Rwanda	Uganda	Kenya
My country has a strong democracy	47.5% (n = 57)	14.4% (n = 18)	60.5% (n = 52)
The leadership in my country is authoritative	47.0% (n = 54)	68.6% (n = 85)	37.3% (n = 32)
News media in my country played a positive role in the country's democratization	65.0% (n = 76)	68.0% (n = 85)	94.2% (n = 81)
The level of press freedom in my country is linked to the strength of democracy in the country	66.9% (n = 77)	55.7% (n = 68)	84.7% (n = 72)

Note. The total number of people who answered these questions in Rwanda ranged from 115 to 120, in Uganda 122 to 125, and in Kenya 85 to 86.

in the country is linked to the strength of democracy). That sentiment was highlighted in our interviews, as well. The former journalist working for the Human Rights Network for Journalists said the media houses who "stood the test of time despite the threats" make a difference, both for journalism and for society: "Those journalists have done a tremendous job . . . the media plays a very central role, actually, as a key pillar of democracy" (Journalist 2, personal communication, June 4, 2018), a sentiment that has been widely noted by others, too.

Scholars have pointed to the integral role that journalists play in democracy-building. As Mukhongo (2010) has suggested, media are "profoundly integral to the democratic process" and "can play a significant role in shaping Africa's political future" (p. 350). And as Table 3.4 showcases, the majority (68%) of Ugandan journalists (as well as the majority of those surveyed in Kenya and Rwanda, 94.2% and 65%, respectively) also believe that news media in the country have played a positive role in democratization. It helps that journalists in Uganda have a fair amount of buy-in from the public.

Ugandan citizens use the radio more than any other medium, and 61% say they "trust completely information heard on the radio" (Twaweza, 2021, p. 1). (Compare this, e.g., to the U.S. where Gallup poll data revealed that just 7% of the public said they trusted the media "a great deal" in 2021 [Brenan, 2021, para. 2]). The next-most trusted news source in Uganda is TV (at 45%), followed by newspapers (23%) and social media (4%). The majority of Ugandan citizens expressed support for press freedom, with 57% saying that "the media should be able to publish without government control" (Twaweza, 2021, p. 2), and between 2013 and 2017, public trust in state-run media by Ugandan citizens decreased from 57% to 40% (Uganda Bureau of Statistics, 2017). When Ugandans did express distrust in the media, it was primarily due to the notion that journalists are poorly compensated and are thus susceptible to bribes (Nassanga & Tayeebwa, 2018).

Overall, Uganda has improved the conditions of its news media sector tremendously in recent decades, especially as the country has continued to gain distance from civil conflict, but as its level of press freedom continues to decline and journalists continue to report complex challenges, it appears the country is experiencing democratic backsliding, as Mukhongo (2010) suggested is happening to other countries in the region. President Museveni's long reign is partly responsible for the decline in media freedoms, but a leader who stays in power for decades cannot be the sole culprit. As we saw in Rwanda, although journalists there face some of the same challenges as journalists in Uganda, that country has seen relatively steady increases in media freedom as the country rebuilds itself and moves further from the genocide against the Tutsi, despite Kagame holding the presidency for more than 20 years. So while Uganda has more distance (in terms of length, scope, and severity) from conflict than Rwanda does, its media ecosystem does not appear to be moving in a linear direction toward more freedoms—in many ways, it is moving backward.

Kalyango and Eckler (2010) assert that "media performance is most successful when its agenda mobilizes citizens to challenge the structures of authoritarian rule by promoting human rights, economic empowerment, and the rule of law" (p. 379). It is yet to be determined whether Uganda's journalists will successfully challenge the authoritarian structures currently in place and move on a path toward democracy or whether the country will slowly slip back into increasingly authoritarian rule. One thing is certain, and Tabaire (2007) put it bluntly: "Only a much more democratic Uganda will ensure a freer press" (p. 208).

4

Kenya

Despite Challenges, Growing Press Freedom in the Gateway to East Africa

The third and final country of focus in this book is Kenya, a unique player in the region. Kenya is the only of the three nations to have coastline, has the largest economy in the region and one of the largest on the continent (behind Egypt, Nigeria, and South Africa), is more competitive in terms of human capital (has higher literacy rates, which come from higher public expenditures on education, larger enrollments in higher education, higher life expectancies, etc.), is considered to have a wider democratic space than its neighbours, and is believed to have the most free and pluralized media system in the region. However, this is not to say the country is flawless. Kenya still faces challenges related to poverty and infrastructure development, government efforts to limit the press, and spurts of politically motivated violence along ethnic lines. Kenya has a multiparty system and has seen five presidents over the same time period as Uganda and Rwanda have each been ruled by the same individual. Even in a country that changes leadership periodically, though, press freedom can ebb and flow.

Perceptions of Press Freedom

Scholars' and Activists' Perspectives

Kenya has a large, vibrant, and sophisticated media system. In the 2022 Reporters Without Borders World Press Freedom Index, Kenya was rated 69 out of 180, which is up substantially since its rating of 102 in 2021 (Reporters Without Borders, 2022a), making Kenya's journalism sector the freest and most stable in the region. The country's "highly-competitive press scene is the most sophisticated in east Africa," credited to constitutional protections, numerous news outlets, bold journalists and public demand for news (BBC,

Press Freedom and the (Crooked) Path Toward Democracy. Meghan Sobel Cohen and Karen McIntyre Hopkinson,
Oxford University Press. © Oxford University Press 2023. DOI: 10.1093/oso/9780197634202.003.0004

2022, para. 6; Harwood et al., 2018). Kenyan media are impactful, including on a policy level, "by raising policymakers' awareness of issues, which leads in many cases to issues being placed on a public policy agenda and in some cases to policy reforms" (Irwin & Kiereini, 2021, p. 171).

Despite its successes, however, Kenyan media have faced challenges with professionalism and sustainability (Obonyo, 2003), training (Okumbe et al., 2017), declining revenues and subsequent layoffs (Harwood et al., 2018), and political influences on coverage (BBC, 2022). Obonyo (2021) also noted the need for the country to develop clearer mechanisms for holding the media accountable. Beyond the challenges and relative media freedoms, though, Reporters Without Borders (2022) noted an environment in which "respect for press freedom in Kenya is highly dependent on the political and economic context" (para. 1). Government restrictions have come in the form of subtle economic, legal, and political pressure and intimidation. Violence is uncommon, as are arrests or killings of journalists. Still, "Covering opposition events or portraying the ruling party and its problems in a negative light can be costly for journalists" (Reporters Without Borders, 2022a, para. 7).

The industry battles with economic challenges as well as professionalism and ethics, especially as they relate to political bias that results from an entrenched entangling of politics and news media (Allen & Gagliardone, 2011; Harwood et al., 2018). Scholars have argued that for as long as Kenyan media have been in existence, people in positions of political or economic power have controlled the media for their own benefit (Ambala, 2014). In the words of Hardwood and colleagues (2017), "Every one of the establishment media houses is owned by either a politician, a close party affiliate, or a business person with commercial interests that depend on politicians' good graces" (p. 12).

Journalists' Perspectives

External measures indicate that Kenya has more press freedom than neighbouring Uganda and Rwanda, and journalists in the country perceive that to be true, despite remaining challenges. In our interviews, an editor/reporter at the commercial Citizen Radio, the largest radio network in Kenya, summarized this shared sentiment: "We feel that they are oppressing us, [but] compared to Rwanda and Uganda we are better off" (Journalist 5, personal communication, February 26, 2019).

In 2019, at the time of our survey, Kenya's Reporters Without Borders press freedom ranking was 100 out of 179, the lowest number of the three countries, indicating the most freedom. Yet still, 44.8% of journalists disagreed with that ranking and felt they had more freedom than the ranking indicated, according to our questionnaire. The same (mis)perception was found in Rwanda. This differed from Uganda, where journalists largely agreed with the international perception that they are restricted. See Rwandan, Ugandan, and Kenyan journalists' levels of agreement with their countries' rankings in Figure 4.1.

In the same survey, we asked how journalists in Rwanda, Uganda, and Kenya perceive the level of press freedom in their respective countries. The data showed that journalists in Kenya reported significantly higher levels of perceived press freedom than journalists in Uganda. They estimated their level of press freedom to be, on average, 66.39 on a scale from 1 to 100 with 100 indicating the most freedom, although not nearly as much as they said they would prefer to have (95.29). Journalists in Uganda estimated their level of press freedom to be about 20 points lower on that scale, while journalists in Rwanda estimated their level of press freedom to be just slightly lower.

Not only did journalists in Kenya perceive their press freedom to be higher than journalists in their neighbouring countries, they also had an optimistic view of their levels of press freedom moving forward. In

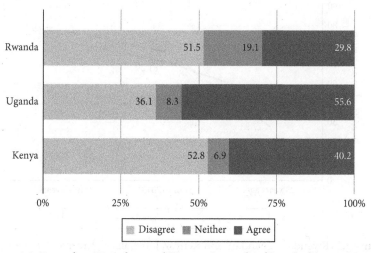

Figure 4.1 Rwandan, Ugandan, and Kenyan Journalists' Level of Agreement With Their Country's 2019 Reporters Without Borders Press Freedom Ranking

10 years (from the time of the 2019 survey), Kenyan journalists predicted their level of press freedom would increase by more than 10 points (to 77.58 out of 100). Rwandan journalists reported a similar optimism, whereas Ugandan journalists predicted their levels of press freedom in 10 years' time would increase by just 3 points. Interestingly, though, journalists in Kenya estimated by far the greatest increase in press freedom over the past quarter-century. They estimated their level of press freedom 25 years ago to be just 27.83—nearly 40 points lower than the present day. Rwandan journalists also perceived their levels of press freedom a quarter-century ago to be significantly lower than present-day levels. This was in sharp contrast to Ugandan journalists, who perceived almost no change in press freedom over the past couple of decades. See the levels of perceived press freedom over time by journalists from all three countries in Figure 4.2.

Kenyan journalists' low levels of perceived freedom 25 years ago can be attributed to President Daniel arap Moi, who ruled the country at the time and maintained total state control over the media. His reign was followed by President Mwai Kibaki, who oversaw the passing of one of the region's most progressive constitutions—which guaranteed a free press—in 2010, explaining the sharp increase in press freedom. This speaks to the massive

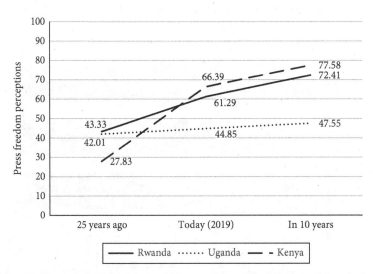

Figure 4.2 Rwandan, Ugandan, and Kenyan Journalists' Perceived Level of Press Freedom Over Time

Note. 0 = no freedom; 100 = full freedom.

influence that a political leader has on a country's media freedoms. Indeed, in our interviews with journalists, they commonly spoke about how press freedom has waxed and waned based on who the president is, among other variables.

Factors That Have Hurt—and Helped—Press Freedom

Although journalists from all three countries—Rwanda, Uganda, and Kenya—ranked a fear of government retaliation and repressive national laws as the most important factors impacting press freedom in our survey, the particular ways journalists are restricted, or supported, vary. Our interview data in Kenya revealed specific factors that have contributed to the rise or fall of press freedom over the years. See the list of journalists we interviewed in Table 4.1.

Media Freedoms Change Alongside the Presidency

When describing changing tides in press freedom throughout the country's history, a reporter at *Business Daily*, a commercial newspaper published by Nation Media Group, summarized the situation: "It all begins with the president" (Journalist 9, personal communication, February 27, 2019).

Ireri et al. (2019) classify the evolution of the country's press into four periods: the colonial era (1895–1962), the post-independence era (1963–1990), the multiparty era (1991–2000) and the digital media era (2002–present). Since independence, Kenya has had five presidents—Jomo Kenyatta (1964–1978), Daniel arap Moi (1978–2002), Mwai Kibaki (2002–2013), Uhuru Kenyatta (2013–2022), and William Ruto elected in September 2022—and each has made a mark on the press.

Jomo Kenyatta's presidency involved a gradual effort to control the media under the guise of nation building (Ogola, 2011b). After the president's fallout with his former deputy, he grew increasingly intolerant of opposition and used the media to delegitimize adversaries in the interest of development. "The state found development journalism particularly consistent with its nation-building project, which had become a convenient euphemism for Kenyatta's regime building. This project gradually led to the cooption of the mainstream news media by the state" (Ogola, 2011b, p. 80). Essentially, the

Table 4.1 Kenya: Interviewee, Job Title, Employer, and Type of Organization

Participant	Job Title	Employer	Type of Org.
Journalist 1	Editor	MT Kenya Star	Commercial
Journalist 2	News anchor/sub-editor	Hot 96 FM	Commercial
Journalist 3	Reporter	The Standard	Commercial
Journalist 4	Sub-editor	Taifa Leo	Commercial
Journalist 5	Editor/reporter	Citizen Radio	Commercial
Journalist 6	Editor	The Standard	Commercial
Journalist 7	Reporter	Taifa Leo	Commercial
Journalist 8	Reporter/News Anchor	NTV	Commercial
Journalist 9	Reporter	Business Daily	Commercial
Journalist 10	Deputy News Editor	People Daily	Commercial
Journalist 11	Magazine/Features Editor	People Daily	Commercial
Journalist 12	Sub-editor	People Daily	Commercial
Journalist 13	Revise Editor	People Daily	Commercial
Journalist 14	Reporter	Daily Nation	Commercial
Journalist 15	Reporter	KTN News	Commercial
Journalist 16	Reporter	The Standard	Commercial
Journalist 17	Reporter	The Nairobian	Commercial
Journalist 18	Editor	NTV	Commercial
Journalist 19	Reporter	Daily Nation	Commercial
Journalist 20	Managing Editor	Citizen Radio	Commercial
Journalist 21	Reporter	China Daily*	Government
Journalist 22	Bureau Chief	People Daily	Commercial
Journalist 23	Reporter	Radio Amani	Religious
Journalist 24	Presenter	Taach FM Radio	Commercial
Journalist 25	Presenter	Radio Waumini	Religious
Journalist 26	Chief News Editor	KBC	Government
Journalist 27	Associate Editor	Nairobi Business Monthly	Commercial
Journalist 28	Reporter	Kibera News Network	Community
Journalist 29	Digital Reporter	CNN*	Commercial
Journalist 30	Editor-in-chief	KBC	Government
Journalist 31	Reporter	Voice of America*	Government
Journalist 32	Reporter/News Anchor	BBC*	Gov./ Commercial
Journalist 33	Reporter	Habari Kibra	Community

* Foreign news outlet (not headquartered in the country where the interview occurred)

media's role was to promote a narrative of national unity. At the time, this was a model used in many African countries (Ogola, 2011b).

After Kenyatta's death, Moi took office, and his presidency was the most oppressive. An associate editor at *Nairobi Business Monthly* said, "It was a dictatorial regime because Moi was holding on to power and he had been through a coup attempt which hardened his stance against freedoms. So he had really emasculated the media" (Journalist 27, personal communication, March 2, 2019). Although press freedom was mentioned in the constitution, the government could still control the media "in the interest of public morality, public order, and national security," and "the interpretation of these provisions was often notoriously ambiguous" (Ogola, 2011b, p. 82). News editors were threatened and detained. Moi launched a national party newspaper, and he and his inner circle bought shares in the two major newspapers, *The Standard* and *The Nation*—in present day, the Moi family "and other close associates own over 90% stake in the Standard Group, Kenya's second-biggest media house" (Business Today, 2018, para. 3). By the early 1990s, the nation faced economic and political decline, and politicians started funding media houses to criticize Moi's administration—a trend that continues today. The president's law to be a one-party state was undone, and the revival of political pluralism sparked a liberalization of the media. It was at this time that the media shifted away from their developmental focus and toward a market-oriented model. Still, the government maintained control of the media by buying the largest share of ads, resulting in (self)censorship by journalists so as not to lose ad revenue (Ogola, 2011b). We still see this today, not only in Kenya but in Uganda and Rwanda as well.

Disillusioned from the Moi regime, a new government was elected in 2002, with Kibaki at the helm. And with that change, eventually, came increased freedoms for journalists. "Because people who fought Moi all through had come to appreciate the role of the media in society when they came to power—and I am talking about former President Mwai Kibaki—they were under obligation to let the media operate freely," said an associate editor at the commercial outlet *Nairobi Business Monthly* (Journalist 27, personal communication, March 6, 2019). At least eventually. The first years of Kibaki's presidency included lapses in journalistic ethics and integrity, post-election violence following his first term, and laws that suppressed broadcast media (Harwood et al., 2018; Ogola, 2011b)—these laws, along with others passed in recent years, have been called punitive and repressive (Oriare & Mshindi, 2008; Ugangu, 2012). But in the end the media saw much leeway, largely as a result of the new constitution passed in 2010, which eliminated existing regulations, guaranteed press freedom and access to information, and transferred significant power from the federal level to the local level. "The Mwai Kibaki regime is considered the best in terms of media freedom . . . People were free to criticize, air opinions, raise issues, investigate matters to do with corruption and all that because he himself was in the forefront of all those things," said the revise editor (which is concerned with quality assurance) at *People Daily* (Journalist 13, personal communication, February 27, 2019), a free ad-supported newspaper that is based in Nairobi and owned by Mediamax Network Ltd. Mediamax is a Kenyan media company associated with former President Uhuru Kenyatta and his family. Though the company has declined to clarify the size of Kenyatta's shareholding (Bloomberg, 2014), a reporter at *Daily Nation* said, "everyone knows [People Daily] is owned by the [then] President [Kenyatta]" (Journalist 19, personal communication, February 28, 2019).

When Kenyatta took office, the state regained control of the media through several amendments passed by parliament (Harwood et al., 2018), and journalists noticed the effects. "Since Kibaki left power in 2013, things have been changing, sliding back into what we call here the 'dark days,' the dark days of the 80s and the 90s," a revise editor at *People Daily* said (Journalist 13, personal communication, February 27, 2019). A magazine/features editor at *People Daily,* the free, ad-supported newspaper with ties to former President Kenyatta, echoed that statement: "Since the [Kenyatta] government got into power, that is in 2013, we have not—it's like the press freedom we enjoyed previously has been reducing, it's like the media is much more constrained now, or they much more muffled than it was before" (Journalist 11, personal communication, February 27, 2019). When President Ruto was elected he criticized the media for biased reporting, but vowed to uphold the nation's press freedom laws and welcomed criticism of his administration when they "go wrong" (Musau, 2022, para. 6).

It's clear that since its independence, the president of Kenya has significantly impacted media freedom in the country. Through legislation and also through political, and at times personal, will, each leader has sprung the media forward or jolted it back. The progression of press freedom has not been a steady, upward trajectory. Rather, it's bounced up and down like the arms of a puppet, controlled by the president at the time and his administration.

Press Freedom Regresses After Post-Election Violence[*]

Just as the election of a nation's president or the passing of a law can affect the state of press freedom, sometimes causing it to rise and fall acutely, so can other specific events that are directly related to such political change. Post-election violence is one such contributing factor in Kenya.

In December 2007, Kenya held an election that some say was rigged in favor of President Kibaki (Bloomfield, 2008). Election observers found that fraud and vote-tampering were used to keep the existing government in power, leading the opposition party and its supporters to reject the results and vow to inaugurate leader Raila Odinga (Rice, 2007). Two months of fighting in communities across the country left more than 1,000 people dead and up to 500,000 people displaced (Human Rights Watch, 2008). News media, and vernacular radio stations in particular (those that broadcast in indigenous languages), were accused of escalating the post-election violence by airing implicit and explicit messages that elevated certain political perspectives and fanned the flames of anger and violence (Ismail & Deane, 2008; Mäkinen & Wangu Kuira, 2008). Specifically, some vernacular radio broadcasts used dehumanizing language such as referring to other ethnic groups as "animals from the West" who must be taken out before they take over "our Kingdom," and mainstream and international media oversimplified the complex political situation as merely ethnic violence (Musungu, 2008).

After the post-election violence, the International Criminal Court indicted radio broadcaster Joshua Sang for alleged crimes against humanity for coordinating a campaign of killing (Arseneault, 2013). However, during the trial, Sang's lawyer argued that he could not have committed such crimes because of a ban on live broadcasts imposed by the Kenyan government, which Sang's station (Kass FM) obliged (Wangui, 2014). Sang's trial was halted due to a lack of evidence; International Criminal Court prosecutors alleged widespread witness tampering, and judges said the trial may be reopened if additional evidence is found (Coalition for the International Criminal Court, n.d.). Despite Sang not being convicted, his defense team's claim of innocence due to the Kenyan government's ban on live broadcasts presents an interesting situation.

*Portions of this subsection were published in Sobel Cohen, M., & McIntyre, K. (2020). Local-Language Radio Stations in Kenya: Helpful or Harmful? *African Journalism Studies*, 40(3), 73–88.

Immediate and long-term censorship occurred in the years that followed the violence in varying ways, including technically, legally, and ideologically. In terms of technical censorship, a reporter at Habari Kibra, a community news outlet operating in the Kibera community in Nairobi (known as the largest urban slum in Africa), explained that their radio station was not able to broadcast because power was cut to the station after the elections and the ensuing violence.

> Then elections came in 2007 and you guys remember what happened, we fought ethnic war. So that destabilized us as a station, like, for around three months, because power was disconnected because of the ethnic divisions within communities in Kenya. (Journalist 33, personal communication, March 8, 2019)

Legally, in 2013, the Kenyan government adopted a multipronged censorship strategy—including regulation, the presence of a strong security state, and the willingness of Kenyans to self-censor—in the name of ensuring peaceful elections (Bowman & Bowman, 2016). And ideologically, journalists and media houses followed suit, choosing to self-censor in order to avoid inciting violence. According to news reporter Jason Straziuso (2013),

> Kenya's Media Owners Association told The Associated Press that media leaders made a "gentleman's agreement" to balance the national interest and the public's right to know, including not reporting anything that could incite ethnic tensions and not airing political statements live. (para. 2)

More recently, the human rights organization Article 19 wrote:

> Journalists who covered the 2017 general elections worked in an exceptionally challenging environment. Attacks against them showed a marked rise in severity and in numbers during [the] prolonged elections period that saw journalists face physical attacks, arrest, being denied access to areas, and receiving various forms of threats, even more so after the August elections and in the run up to the October repeat presidential poll. (2018, p. 4)

A reporter at *Taifa Leo*, a Swahili-language newspaper published by Nation Media Group, contextualized this situation:

[The amount of press freedom] has been shifting and I think it shifts usually because of the political environment. When the political environment is favorable, then journalists, the fourth estate, we have much more
freedom. But when it is hostile, and hostile either because of the political figureheads or because of local politics . . . political disputes among
mwananchi [ordinary citizens] . . . you would need to take precautions
because you might get sucked into [the disputes] and they might want you
to choose a side. . . . The media are always in the center and you have to get
fires from all sides. But when the environment is calm and, like, now we
have a calmness . . . we have not heard anybody shouting that "you guys are
doing bad press, why are you doing this?" No. But I'm sure it's because of
the calmness. . . . So yes, there is press freedom but it is dependent on the
political environment. (Journalist 7, personal communication, February
27, 2019)

Entangled Relationship Between Politicians and the Press Provokes Self-Censorship

Post-election violence has acutely affected press freedom in Kenya, but ideological differences linger and impact press freedom—particularly through
self-censorship—in more persistent and subtle ways. This is largely blamed
on the fact that politicians in the country are deeply entangled with the
news media.

"Almost every prominent politician in this country owns one media house
or another," the revise editor at *People Daily* said (Journalist 13, personal
communication, February 27, 2019). Several journalists in our interviews
talked about this. They described how politicians, or the politically ambitious, will become majority shareholders in an existing media house or
launch their own media house, especially vernacular radio stations, because
it's the easiest way to spread their message. "Basically for any politician to
get ahead and to have their own mouthpiece to spread their propaganda to
the public, they think of setting up a media house or radio station," said a
deputy news editor at *People Daily* (Journalist 10, personal communication,
February 27, 2019).

This happens at especially high rates in the lead-up to elections,
explained a reporter/news anchor at NTV, a TV station owned by Nation
Media Group:

> Someone decides, "I want to vie for this position, governor, senator; I need a channel whereby I can be using to pass my messages." So they come up with a radio station. Right now we have so many politicians who are coming up with radio stations, TV stations, in preparation for the next general election. So I think if I start quoting I can quote more than 20 of them with their media houses. (Journalist 8, personal communication, February 27, 2019)

Politicians think if they cannot get the support of any other media house, at least their own media house will stand with them, our interviewees said. And these partisan media outlets are often divided on tribal lines. "The tendency is that you'll bring in the management of your trusted people, [and] the trusted quite often will end up coming from maybe your tribesmen or -women," explained an editor at NTV (Journalist 18, personal communication, February 28, 2019). In a country with at least 42 ethnic groups/tribes (Balaton-Chrimes, 2021), this problem is widespread. "Politicians at every level of government have used ethnic allegiances as a tool to mobilize support" (Harwood et al., 2018, p. 6), and a member of parliament's tribal affiliation was one of the strongest predictors of newspaper coverage (Ireri, 2012). Tribal loyalty can be strong, to the point that journalists and others support the politician or political candidate who aligns with their tribe even if they do not agree with that person's platform, our interviewees said.

But no matter whether a journalist is from the same tribe as his or her media house's owner or not, these tribal allegiances and competitions affect editorial independence, journalists said. A Nairobi-based digital reporter for CNN explained:

> Once you have the politicians own or even have a share in the media, then they control the narrative. . . . You'll only report on what they want to be reported. Like you just can't go outside the box, it's like within the prison of what they want. (Journalist 29, personal communication, March 6, 2019)

The revise editor at *People Daily* gave an example of how self-censorship plays out in this scenario:

> For example, when you do investigative stories sometimes [journalists] would retreat when you realize the person you're investigating is probably

your boss or someone who sits on your boss or a friend of your boss, so there are those challenges in this country. (Journalist 13, personal communication, February 27, 2019)

These quotes and existing research make it clear that these political and ethnic biases, and the accompanying concentration of media ownership along political and ethnic lines, affects news coverage (Harwood et al., 2018; Mbeke et al., 2010; Simiyu, 2013, 2014), and particularly impacts political news coverage (Cheeseman et al., 2019; Makokha, 2010).

This type of media control, brought on by ideological differences, does not limit press freedom as overtly as laws or other factors discussed in this book, but the self-censorship that results from it undoubtedly impacts critical and fair news reporting in Kenya.

Specific Factors Push Kenya's Press Freedom Ahead of Its Neighbours

International Connections Elevate Media

Despite ups and downs in press freedom based on the political climate and tribal tensions, Kenyan media experience more freedom than their neighbours. Interview data reveal that Kenya, referred to colloquially as "The gateway to Africa" (Mulligan, 2015), has intentionally cultivated links to the West. Many journalists in the country commented on the relationships, treaties, and shared norms between Kenya and other countries, particularly Western countries, that contribute to the Kenyan mediascape having more freedoms. A presenter at Radio Waumini, a radio station owned and operated by the Kenya Conference of Catholic Bishops, explained that the country's media freedoms come from international treaties. "Again the international treaties, Kenya is linked to so many international treaties focusing on media" (Journalist 25, personal communication, March 5, 2019). Similarly, a Kenya-based BBC reporter and news anchor explained the strategic role that Kenya plays in the world but also the role that Kenyan leaders have played in developing and reacting to international norms:

Relationships with the West can be viewed from different perspectives because from an international relations background it might tell you, because Kenya is a strategic country in terms of, it has the coastline, it is a good place to maybe even monitor the Horn of Africa or even the Middle East as opposed to, let's say, Uganda which is landlocked, first of all, and Tanzania, which is further south. But also I think it is the relationship of individual Kenyan leaders—a number of them studied abroad in the West, a number of them were friends of current leaders of Western countries. So then there are the fingerprints of colonization because Kenya was like the headquarters of the East African British Protectorate. So this is where the Brits monitored affairs of Uganda and Kenya and the Great Lakes region. (Journalist 32, personal communication, March 8, 2019)

Similarly, the revise editor at *People Daily* also explained how the nation's location plays a role in relationship building:

Since independence, 1963, I think Kenya has been in bed with the West more than the other countries. There is Britain, you know we were colonized by Britain, so there is that—the residual part of Britain, most of the things you'll find, even our parliamentary system, we took from Britain. So the links with the West, mostly Europe and America of course, those links, there has been a tendency to go the Western way. And then Kenya is strategically placed . . . military wise . . . when there are conflicts in the region, the West sends troops to Kenya. You have Americans, they have a military camp in Mombasa, at the coast, because of the terrorism in Somalia and such things. Now this interaction, there has been a deliberate effort from the West to ensure that Kenya is stable. So you find all the media houses, all the international media houses, CNN, BBC in Africa, they are based here in Nairobi. So if you want to go to DRC [the Democratic Republic of the Congo], you go and report in DRC, then come back here. So that support from the West has enabled an element of stability here. (Journalist 13, personal communication, Feb. 27, 2019)

A news anchor and sub-editor at Hot 96 FM, a Nairobi-based commercial radio station owned by Royal Media Services, elaborated on these international linkages, explaining how bilateral relationships in all of their forms (political, economic, etc.) contribute to increased freedoms:

I believe it is all about relationships that we have out there, bilateral ties, it always goes down to that. Because if the business environment thrives, then definitely more countries will be interested in us. There are so many prospects in Kenya—there are minerals, there are national parks, there are tourists' sites, there are things that people from other countries would love to come and see, the giraffes and whatnot. So for us to actually make that happen, then the government has to draw the line; at some point it has to draw the line. If freedom of expression is something that's being curtailed at this very stage and there are countries that believe in freedom of expression then definitely the [Kenyan] government is going to have a problem there. So I believe it is all about the bilateral relationships that we have—that's what is building Kenya to where it is today. (Journalist 2, personal communication, February 25, 2019)

Many of these international linkages have contributed to Kenya's political and media advancements—and the nation's ability to be a "trendsetter" in the region—according to journalists. "I think Kenyan media right now is also a trendsetter [in the region] just like mpesa [mobile money] because [of] the things that happen here. I was in the U.S. last November and we visited CNN, we visited other community radio stations, whatever happens here is whatever happens in the U.S.," said a managing editor at Citizen Radio (Journalist 20, personal communication, March 1, 2019), a commercial radio station which, as of early 2022, was the most listened-to radio station in the country, with a 10.2% share of the nation's radio audience (Kibuacha, 2022). Similarly, a reporter for *Taifa Leo* explained that Kenya has media freedom:

Because of the exposure to the international media and international world, moreso because we are like a gateway into Eastern and Central Africa. And so that helps with an influx of knowledge and experiences from outside and a mixture of cultures and all that. . . . That helps to bring in different perspectives, so you don't have just one, let's say, one routine, one angle, one way of doing things but you have a mixture because of the inflow of different peoples and different cultures and the exposure. So that exposure helps us in Kenya a bit more than Rwanda. (Journalist 7, personal communication, February 27, 2019)

Similarly, the reporter/news anchor from NTV explained why Kenya is a leader in Africa and the region:

[Kenyans] feel they understand their rights, that they feel they're more entitled as compared to any other person in the region, because of the way the world has also looked at the region and felt like Kenya is like the entry point to East Africa. When you look at the number of tourists who come to Kenya they are more than any other country. We have so many people who want to come to Africa but they land in Kenya first then they move to that other place. So that has given Kenya that feel that we are the most powerful. And then the fact that the Kenyan economy is stronger than any other economy in the region, that it makes Kenya feel, we are stronger. So for that reason you realize that we don't want to be compared to other countries, we feel other people are not having freedom, Kenya we'll want to have that freedom. (Journalist 8, personal communication, February 27, 2019)

As a result of this power, a reporter for commercial station Kenya Television Network (KTN) News said Kenyan media have significant influence:

If there is anything happening in the region, for Kenya it creates an impact if the story is covered in the Kenyan media more than it is covered in the regional media. Like, I think, last year when [President of South Sudan] Salva Kiir was negotiating with [First Vice President of South Sudan] Riek Machar so that they can have a coalition government for him to come back, the stories that were being carried, and I covered some of them, they were pulling more interest here than in South Sudan. And they would actually tell us and brief us everything which was happening from Juba. . . . So even in terms of how we cover stories, we are always seen like we are the pacesetters for the region—Uganda, Rwanda, Burundi; what Kenya says has more impact. (Journalist 15, personal communication, February 28, 2019)

Kenya's international linkages extend beyond the West. Many journalists spoke about China's growing influence in the region and how such a linkage presents unique challenges and opportunities for local media systems. The revise editor at *People Daily*, for example, spoke about lessening Western influence on free expression during U.S. President Donald Trump's time in office and a resulting increase in Chinese influence:

When we look at those people called "developmental partners," for example, Britain, the United States of America, France . . . when it comes to freedom, especially the U.S., like the Trump administration has been a disappointment, you find it's an administration that is more friendly to people like [Rwandan President] Kagame, people like [Ugandan President]

Museveni, [former president] Duterte in Philippines. So you find that, for example, when there used to be media oppression here [in Kenya] you would find Washington is talking, London is talking, everybody is talking [in opposition to the media oppression] . . . those voices have gone down. So what you'd call "developmental partners," mostly from the West, they've diminished. And in doing so there is another monster that has risen called China which has no time for media freedom. So when you have Chinese all over . . . and Washington is quiet, London is quiet . . . there is, for ex-ample, an element of consciousness that repression is going on the rise in Africa. . . . When there's that silence, it carries a lot. (Journalist 13, personal communication, February 27, 2019)

China had a notable footprint in Africa in the 1950s and 1960s and is working to (re)build its influence based on the nation's current and long-term goals (Alden et al., 2008; Chaudhury, 2021). One component of China's "Going Out Strategy" has been to increase the presence of Chinese state-owned media, specifically Xinhua (China's news agency), China Global Television Network (CGTN), China Radio International, and *China Daily*, across the African continent, along with wiring media content free of charge, offering scholarships to African journalism students, and providing tech-nical assistance to African broadcasters (Chaudhury, 2021). This influence is seen across the continent, including in East Africa.

The African branch of CGTN is headquartered in Nairobi along with a regional Xinhua bureau. *China Daily* publishes from its offices in Nairobi and Johannesburg, and China Radio International has a station in Nairobi that broadcasts across the country (Mwakideu, 2021). Pro-China articles from Xinhua have been "widely adopted" by English-language newspapers in Kenya. The Kenyan Broadcasting Corporation is accused of portraying a November 2019 article praising China's efforts to eradicate poverty as locally generated content when it was a Xinhua-produced story (Chaudhury, 2021, para. 10).

However, Kenyan journalists and media houses have not accepted all of China's help and media content without skepticism. Journalist Chrispin Mwakideu quotes Joseph Odindo, a former editor at Kenya's Nation Media Group, as he explained:

"We had a serious disagreement with them when we published an inves-tigative report on Kenya's SGR railway project funded by China," Odindo noted. The investigative story examined the difficult process of building the railway and how it cost vast sums of tax-payers money to simply maintain it. "The Chinese Embassy and their communications manager canceled all their advertisements with The Standard and withdrew the supplement," Odindo said. "They demanded that we had to stop negative coverage." (Mwakideu, 2021, para. 17–19)

Empowered Citizens Advocate for Press Freedom

Another factor that journalists said has facilitated press freedom in Kenya is its empowered civil society, which stems from a number of factors, including both a space for dissent given by public officials and the culture and spirit of Kenyans which has promoted the growth of human rights including media freedoms. A managing editor at Citizen Radio in Kenya said that Kenyans like to talk and that that, alone, has contributed to a culture of rights:

> I think it's just the culture because Kenyans like talking. Kenyans they always meet and you'll find them talking for hours. . . . There's even one CEO who came here and said Kenya is a peculiar country because of the way it communicates. (Journalist 20, personal communication, March 1, 2019)

A reporter and news anchor at the BBC in Nairobi provided context as to how and why Kenyans may be vocal in advocating for their rights:

> Even way before colonization, when we had chiefdoms and small kingdoms in Kenya, Kenya was a vibrant trading partner with the Middle East, with Far East Asian countries, and we benefited from education, from business. So even by the time the colonialists were here, more Kenyans were educated and more Kenyans knew or were aware of individual rights. Because individual rights is not something we attained through the constitution, it is not something we attained through independence. That's why we were fighting colonialism—we were fighting colonialism because we were aware that our rights had been taken away by these people, because our land was on the line. So I think it is a number of factors that have helped Kenya position itself as a "democratic or rights center" for East Africa. (Journalist 32, personal communication, March 8, 2019)

Similarly, a presenter at the commercial radio station Taach FM said the country has an "enlightened public that also believes in their rights" (Journalist 24, personal communication, March 2, 2019). This belief that the public has in their rights extends to media rights. "In fact one of the defenders of press freedom is the Kenyan public because they really believe that the media is there to guard our post," said an editor at *The Standard* (Journalist 6, personal communication, February 27, 2019), a newspaper with one of the largest readerships in the country, following behind the *Daily Nation* (Media Council of Kenya, 2020). As mentioned above, the Moi family holds shares in the company that owns *The Standard*, and, as an editor at MT Kenya Star said, *The Standard* is "technically" independent but is "owned by the family of the retired President, Moi[;] they are the majority shareholders" (Journalist 1, personal communication, February 25, 2019).

Journalists explained that the public has considered the media their most trusted institution, and so they fight for them. And this public trust in media in Kenya has been documented by researchers as well. According to the Reuters Institute for the Study of Journalism's 2021 Digital News Report:

> Trust in media is relatively high by international standards, with 61% saying they trust most news most of the time. By contrast, trust is lower in the news found in social media or search engines. KTN News, Citizen TV, The Daily Nation, and NTV are the most trusted sources of news. (Gicheru, 2021, para. 12)

Interestingly, despite lower public trust in social media, in recent years it has become the main source of news and information for Kenyans—overtaking radio, TV, and newspapers (Mwita, 2021). This is understandable, given that the median age in the country is 20.1 years as of 2020 (Worldometer, 2020, as cited in Mwita, 2021).

In Uganda and Rwanda, countries with similarly young populations, public trust in the media is also relatively high but arguably more complex. As discussed in Chapter 2, in Rwanda, the media betrayed the public during the 1994 genocide against the Tutsi, and that has affected public trust in the media today, although the impact is unclear. Some research has found that journalists believe they are viewed as villains and not to be trusted, because of their role in the genocide (Moon, 2021), while other research conducted among members of the public found that the public strongly trusts the media, especially government media, precisely because the man who runs the government today (President Paul Kagame) helped end the genocide (McIntyre & Sobel Cohen, 2021). As discussed in Chapter 3, in Uganda, the public reports strong trust in information received on the radio, followed by television content, but reports less, and declining, trust in newspapers and social media content (Twaweza, 2021).

Despite public trust in media remaining relatively high in Kenya, that is not to say that Kenyans passively accept media content. In addition to advocating for media and fighting for press freedom, a reporter at the commercial *Daily Nation*, the most read newspaper in Kenya (Media Council of Kenya, 2020), explained how the Kenyan public simultaneously holds news media accountable:

> There's also the Kenyan spirit. I'm sure you've heard about how Kenyans called out the *New York Times* for using some inappropriate pictures [posted after the Dusit D2 terrorist attack], pictures that Kenyans felt were inappropriate and Kenyans really came out. So I think within those freedoms and those privileges it has also emboldened our spirits, it has taught us to be more courageous, to be able to stand up to people who they might feel are not doing the right thing. And this is not just against government because you also need to realize that Kenyans are also—they don't just stand up to international media, they also stand up to local media. (Journalist 19, personal communication, February 28, 2019)

The public understands that the entangled relationships between media house owners and politicians influence news coverage and this causes mistrust (Harwood et al., 2018). But they are not afraid to speak up about it, the reporter from the *Daily Nation* explained:

> [Kenyans'] tolerance for bullshit, sorry to use that word, is very, very low. A small typo here or there, it's all over Twitter and all that, and they interrogate our stories, they interrogate the angles of our stories. So you can say there's a lot of consciousness and there's a lot of—there's a remarkably high level of media literacy within the Kenyan population compared to other countries. Because they consume media, they are voracious consumers of newspapers whether online or physical newspapers. And these are the

kind of people who are aware of what they deserve from the media, what they deserve from the newspaper, so I think it's a Kenyan thing. Somebody once said that Kenyans are peculiar and it's true that Kenyans are very peculiar characters. And we are not afraid of calling you out, it doesn't matter if you're African or Mzungu [foreigner]. (Journalist 19, personal communication, February 28, 2019)

However, Kenyans have not always been so vocal. A managing editor at Citizen Radio said that Kenyans are very communicative, but were less expressive when there was a one-party state:

I remember one-party state when you could not even talk ill against the government because you thought the walls were listening. But when it was opening up then everybody started being free. Kenyans just talk about anything and everything, even things that they don't know, and I think that has really helped in the democratization of this country because people will always give feedback. So it's culture if you ask me—people are willing to express themselves. (Journalist 20, personal communication, March 1, 2019)

This raises the chicken-and-egg question. Were Kenyans naturally empowered, or did they become so only after they were afforded more free speech?

Either way, the Kenyan spirit, the country's links to the Western world, the multi-party political system, and lack of civil conflict—all of these contribute to the state of press freedom in the country today. The Kenyan journalists that we surveyed and interviewed were confident that they fared better than their neighbours in terms of press freedom, democracy, and development (and by almost all measures, they do). They repeatedly described press freedom as being highest in their country compared to Uganda and Rwanda, and they were equally optimistic about their country's path toward a strong democracy. They were less likely than journalists in Uganda and Rwanda to feel that the leadership in their country is authoritative. They were more likely to believe their country has a strong democracy, and they were most likely to believe the level of press freedom in their country is linked to the strength of democracy in the country. Finally, they were the most likely to believe that journalists in their country have contributed to the nation's strengthening democracy. See Table 3.4.

Yet, Kenya's path toward increasing democracy and press freedom has not been linear. As discussed, media freedoms have been rocked, particularly when authoritative presidents have taken charge and, more recently, when spurts of violence occur after elections. In Kenya, we see again how a nation's political and cultural history and present-day situation, including deliberately curated bilateral ties as well as the personality and nature of citizens, impacts its press freedom. Such context is vital to accurately evaluating press freedom. In Chapter 5, we summarize the factors that should be considered when understanding press freedom and media development in developing nations.

5

Democracy's Hiccups

Factors That Regress and Progress Press Freedom

Chapter 1 provided an overview of the media histories in Rwanda, Uganda, and Kenya and examined relevant existing frameworks that seek to explain media systems and press freedom landscapes in developing nations. Chapters 2 through 4 took a deep look at the three nations under study and highlighted unique elements that impact press freedom in those countries. Building upon those insights, this chapter takes a step back and pulls out commonalities across nations that highlight specific factors that can regress and progress press freedom in East Africa. While these factors emerged from research in East Africa, they are broad enough to be examined as possible contributing elements of media systems in other regions of the world. This chapter examines yardsticks, if you will, for political and press freedom change—in essence, specific political and development-related events, processes, or structures that journalists say impact their freedoms.

As such, this chapter puts forth a set of factors that can be used to understand media systems in developing nations from a more historically and contextually informed view, according to the journalists that we interviewed and surveyed. The following examples are specific factors commonly mentioned by journalists in the region that highlight how certain events or systems can promote, slow, alter, or derail development and democratization, and in turn improve or lessen levels of press freedom: distance from conflict, political benchmarks (specifically, who is in office and for how long, elections and their aftermath, political and tribal influences on media ownership, and how laws are interpreted and enforced), international linkages, and the strength of a country's civil society (including nongovernmental organizations, social norms, and journalism cultures). While these factors are certainly not the only elements that can influence mediascapes in varying countries, this list can be understood as a starting point for nuanced understanding and theorizing about press freedom environments operating within varying political systems.

Press Freedom and the (Crooked) Path Toward Democracy. Meghan Sobel Cohen and Karen McIntyre Hopkinson, Oxford University Press. © Oxford University Press 2023. DOI: 10.1093/oso/9780197634202.003.0005

Variables That Impact Press Freedom Based on Conversations with Journalists

Distance From Conflict

In the previous chapters of this book, much has been written about the evolution of the press after a conflict. Journalists that we spoke to, as well as
scholars and activists, have noted that the genocide against the Tutsi in
Rwanda and Uganda's fight against the Lord's Resistance Army (LRA) have
each resulted in government crackdowns on the press, to varying degrees,
at different times; and this was also seen on a smaller scale during and after
post-election violence, terrorist attacks, and a battle against al-Shabaab in
Kenya. Of course, the severity of press suppression will undoubtedly change
based on the scope and length of the conflict, so in essence, both the distance
from conflict as well as the harshness of the conflict are at play.

Two-thirds (66.9%) of journalists from the three countries in our survey
agreed or strongly agreed that the level of press freedom improves as the
country moves further away from social/ethnic conflict (war, genocide, political or tribal conflict, etc.). This quantitative finding aligns closely with
explicit and implicit results from interviews with the journalists as well as
in secondary literature. Some of the interviewed journalists spoke directly
about the level of press freedom improving as the country moved beyond
conflict, and others spoke more generally, with those in Kenya expressing
much more freedom of expression, those in Uganda a bit less, and those in
Rwanda notably less, which aligns with the distance that their respective
countries have from conflict.

As discussed in Chapter 3, Uganda has experienced conflict with the LRA
which contributed to the viewpoint of government leadership that some
journalists may represent the opposition, and thus, stricter regulations
need to be enacted. As the conflict lessened, so too did some of the media
restrictions, at least temporarily—many journalists spoke about the
restrengthening of restrictions as time passed. However, the ideology that
government officials should not trust journalists and should not be forthcoming with information has maintained even though restrictions have
ebbed and flowed.

Other scholars have noted that in Kenya, journalists have been attacked
and prosecuted for writing (sometimes on their own Facebook pages) about

conflict and/or military-related topics such as the killing of Kenyan soldiers in the war with al-Shabaab (Einashe, 2016). Similarly, after terrorist attacks in Kenya at the Westgate mall, Garissa University, and DusitD2 hotel, a climate of self-censorship has grown as editors opt to "either give objective, but limited coverage to terrorism or chose to go with official versions out of fear of reprisals if they highlight something the government does not want" (Muindi, 2020, p. 10). A drastic increase in threats and attacks on journalists in the country was documented following the terrorist attacks (Einashe, 2016), and the government's counter-terrorism efforts "bore a negative impact on media freedom in Kenya" by limiting the agency of journalists and enacting new laws that restrict the rights of journalists and access to information (Muindi, 2021, p. 103). Some of these restrictions on the press came during and immediately after the conflicts took place and began to lessen as time went on, which aligns with findings from the journalists interviewed and surveyed for this book.

Chapter 2 focused on Rwanda and the role that media played during the genocide against the Tutsi as well as journalists' role in the reconstruction of the country. Many interviewees in Rwanda spoke about necessary limitations that media must operate within as a result of the not-too-distant genocide. As mentioned in Chapter 2, a Kigali-based news editor at *The East African* acknowledged the limitations on press freedom in Rwanda due to the genocide, compared to neighbouring countries which have not had the same level of conflict and/or are further away from it: "We cannot say we operate with the same level of independence as, for instance, our other counterparts in the region, Uganda or Kenya. And again it's because of the history [of genocide]" (Journalist 17, personal communication, June 1, 2016).

Many journalists in Uganda used the Rwandan mediascape as an example or a barometer for how much more freedom they have. A reporter at the commercial TV station NBS in Uganda attributed this, in part, to Rwanda's young private sector which has only (re)arisen after the genocide: "Rwanda's private sector is really young. Their private sector is barely about 15 years. Our private sector is nearly 50 years. So you have established private sector players in the media market who can make decisions" (Journalist 3, personal communication, June 4, 2018). Similarly, a videographer for the BBC in Uganda, who used to work as a reporter in Rwanda, spoke about Rwanda's media being young, given its rebuilding post-genocide, compared to Uganda and Kenya:

It's really still a virgin land, but it is carefully treaded [*sic*] into because of [the genocide] 20-something years ago and because the government has failed to train and, like, make [journalists] now learn from the mistakes [made during the genocide]. . . . They are not yet mature for it. . . . And that's what brings a bigger challenge of press freedom. . . . In 20 years, they'll be where we [Uganda] were 20 years [ago]. . . . We work fast. Kenya works faster than us, because the media in Kenya's like 100 years old. Ours is like 50, 25, actually. . . . But I believe in five years, if [Rwandan journalists] keep up . . . [and] understand what the role of media—right now—is supposed to be doing, if they learn that [they will have more freedoms]. (Journalist 19, personal communication, June 7, 2018)

Journalists in Kenya similarly used both Rwanda and Uganda as markers for the high level of press freedom that they have, with many noting that histories of conflict play a role in each country's media environment. For example, a reporter for *The Standard* in Kenya said:

If you compare Kenya and Uganda and Rwanda, Kenya is very far ahead in terms of press freedom. . . . The media here [in Kenya] is very versatile, very aggressive, they know what they're doing, they know what we are supposed to give to the audience. Uganda is still a bit, there is a lot of control from the government, same as Rwanda. But Rwanda we understand because of what they experienced before—the genocide—so there has been a lot of control in terms of what goes out to the public. (Journalist 3, personal communication, February 26, 2019)

Similarly, a magazine/features editor at *People Daily* in Kenya explained that Kenya likely has more freedom given the lack of war in the country. "If you look at countries that are coming out of war, it means that they're still struggling with issues of democracy . . . and that means press freedom is a challenge in those nations" (Journalist 11, personal communication, February 27, 2019).

Many journalists in Rwanda cautioned that while the press landscape is improving, the genocide is still recent and remains fresh in many people's minds, thus necessitating some limits on the press. A journalist in a management role at the commercial online platform Umuseke in Rwanda explained that the media environment is evolving but still tightly interwoven with lingering impacts from the genocide:

[The media landscape is] changing, of course, from what it used to be, from the unfair side and to be more, even more fair, more free for us. I cannot say the media in Rwanda is free, totally free to talk about anything, and that relates to our old history, bad history. Because if you let the people talk about all of what's in their hearts, it can be explosive. It can really be explosive. So there have to be some guidelines. I really accept that and I don't agree with some journalists who think we can talk about anything we want. But for me, I think we have to have boundaries, so, if that is called freedom of the press, we are not free, totally free. But I agree that we can't be free for anything, because what happened here was too bad to come back again. So we cannot be free, we cannot really be free. Maybe in 100 or 200 years, but for now, no, no, no. . . . I know people who, if you let them publish or talk anything in the radio, can harm the society, very much harm the society and that can be, you know how Rwandans consume media, they think that what we say or what we write is the truth, so, you cannot let the people do what they want just after 22 years [post-genocide]. (Journalist 10, personal communication, May 30, 2016)

Similarly, as discussed in Chapter 2, a senior producer from the commercial station Radio/TV 10 in Rwanda said:

Even if we are having developments in Rwanda . . . people who committed genocide are still there; people who suffered are still there; widows, orphans are still there. They are still having a fresh memory. They are still having fresh wounds. It means that we have to be careful. Because of that, some people do self-censorship. . . . Even if you can't get penalized, you self-censor yourself, you say, "No no no, this is untouchable, I'm not going to talk on this [subject]." (Journalist 4, personal communication, May 28, 2016)

But a journalist in a management function at *The East African* in Uganda was quick to acknowledge the work that journalists in Rwanda are doing to innovate:

[In] Rwanda, the shock of the genocide and a very strong fist of government [is] trying to direct, not just the journalists but entire society [*sic*] interpretation of genocide. Those laws about denying genocide, and then, defining genocide only in a restrictive sense. . . . There are so many controls but . . . I think the interesting thing for me . . . [is] the people trying to

> push back using new forms of social media, online publications in Rwanda.
> I think if you compare what they're doing in Kigali and what we're doing
> here [in Uganda], I think they're doing a lot more incredible work there in a
> much more restricted environment than we have here. (Journalist 27, per-
> sonal communication, June 12, 2018)

Despite reasons to worry about backsliding (discussed in Chapter 2), the
type of innovation mentioned by the Ugandan journalist above, especially
when working within authoritarian systems, may eventually lead to sys-
temic changes. Kenyan journalists spoke about the evolution of their democratic and media spaces, and how these did not come by happenstance,
nor did they occur overnight. For example, an editor at *The Standard*
in Kenya explained that they would trace media freedoms back to the
struggle to expand the democratic space, a struggle that was hard fought.
Those who experienced the one-party state know how hard it was to earn
media freedoms, and they would therefore be hard pressed to give those
freedoms up.

> I would say [Kenya has media freedom] because you have sections of this
> population that witnessed how an authoritarian regime really can be and
> how life can be difficult. . . . And then of course you have a whole new gen-
> eration that has grown, the millennials that have grown in all this freedom
> and Twitter. So you try to tell them you can limit on their freedom, they'll
> come after your neck. (Journalist 6, personal communication, February
> 27, 2019)

In short, we see a macro-level correlation between distance from conflict and press freedom, so the length of time that a country has gone since
civil war/extreme violence is one variable to consider when evaluating a
country's press freedom. However, that alone is not a trustworthy or ade-
quate indicator. In Chapter 2 we discussed why Rwanda's steady climb toward press freedom may not last, and in Chapters 3 and 4 we discussed
the setbacks to media freedoms due to political events and structures. So,
even with increasing democratization and growing distance from conflict,
challenges remain with regard to politics and the press, and journalists
spoke about a number of other factors that also interplay with media
environments.

Political Benchmarks

Building from the previous discussion about a nation's distance from conflict, journalists regularly, and unsurprisingly, mentioned that the political environment in their country (and those around it, and globally) plays a key role in their ability to do their job without government interference. The complicated relationship between politics and the press has been examined and documented in varying capacities for many decades, and was similarly noted by journalists in these three countries. For example, a magazine/features editor at *People Daily* in Kenya explained the links and the complicated nature of democratization and press freedom:

> I think press freedom goes hand in hand with democracy. If a state enjoys democracy, chances are that there's more press freedom. Even as much as we say democracy is a very foreign thing, and I guess our different regimes define democracy differently, but I know they definitely go hand in hand. (Journalist 11, personal communication, February 27, 2019)

However, journalists did not just think that democracy enables more press freedom, but that it could also go the other direction. In the survey data, 73.8% of respondents from the three countries agreed or strongly agreed that news media in their country played a positive role in the country's democratization, and 67.5% agreed or strongly agreed that the level of press freedom in their country is linked to the strength of democracy in the country. A reporter at *Taifa Leo*, a Swahili-language newspaper in Kenya, put it bluntly: "The pattern is that, I think, in Africa the political environment determines press freedom with such a large margin that where there's calmness politically then the press are free" (Journalist 7, personal communication, February 27, 2019). Even with political calmness, though, journalists spoke of a number of factors that complicate the press and political ecosystems.

Length and Scope of Leadership

Journalists in all three countries spoke about the impact that the president's time in office has on media systems[1], though it wasn't always straightforward in that the longer a president is in office, the less press freedom the nation receives (though that can hold true, and may be the case in Uganda). For example, in Kenya, despite having more media freedoms than other nations in the region, journalists still experienced fluctuating media freedoms based on who was in office and for how long (as discussed in Chapter 4). A sub-editor at the commercial newspaper *People Daily* in Kenya explained:

> It will depend on the government that will be in power at the time. Because as you have seen different governments have different rates of freedom. So depending on who will be at the top that will translate across the board. (Journalist 12, personal communication, February 27, 2019)

But this relationship between the media and political transitions can flow in both directions. A Kenya-based reporter at *China Daily*, an English-language newspaper run by the Communist Party of China, explained the varying degrees of freedom in accordance with different presidents but also explained the media's role in promoting political change:

> During the Moi era . . . the people who were agitating at that point for multi-partyism leaned more on the media to highlight the era of the second presidency. So at that point the media was quite instrumental in the country going democratic, on the country actually moving from one party to different parties. And so from then on, actually, I think the political system had to give more leeway to the media. Because the media was fundamental for the democratic space that we got. And unlike Rwanda and Uganda whereby, in Uganda the political system or the presidency hasn't changed . . . even if [press freedom] is actually enshrined in the constitution . . . you wouldn't really expect the media to change because the leadership hasn't changed. When it comes to Rwanda actually the media was actually castigated to have done much towards the genocide that happened. So I would actually say that because of that . . . the leadership approach [press freedom] from what had happened during the genocide. (Journalist 21, personal communication, March 1, 2019)

While Kenya has experienced significant political changes—democratization and backsliding and a shift from a one-party system to a multiparty system—that impact media freedoms, Ugandan journalists operate under a president who has been in power for more than three decades, and Rwandan journalists do so under a president who has been in office for more than 20 years. A reporter for *Taifa Leo* in Kenya noted the impacts of

President Museveni's long tenure in Uganda and how the situation differs in Kenya:

> For Uganda there has been a constant head of state for that long and so there's, like, a stronghold, a stranglehold on everything and that includes press freedom. Unlike here [in Kenya] where the probability of this person who is wielding the—any sort of stranglehold, knows that after, well, the maximum they can go is 10 years and so they will not be here [for extended times like Museveni], so towards the end usually they become flexible and relaxed because they know they're leaving. (Journalist 7, personal communication, February 27, 2019)

Similarly, a Rwandan journalist in a management role at the commercial outlet Great Lakes Voice, which no longer publishes, explained that President Kagame controls the media as one component in directing the narrative surrounding Rwanda's post-genocide development:

> If there is a country where you don't have opposition, in a situation where you don't have human rights organizations working, in a country where freedom of expression is strictly limited and monitored—for the press to survive, it's minimum chances. For me, I would attribute everything that we are on the government. And how does the government do that, to control the narrative, and know what it is you want to hear, they dilute it. They tell you, "Ah, ok, doing business in Rwanda. . . . It's good. It's great. We'll have big houses built." But at what expense does it take to have a great city in Kigali? Where are the street children? Where are the poor? . . . To me, the greatest achievement of this country is not the recovery and everything; it is the effort to control the narrative. You have to be good at it. Really good. (Journalist 23, personal communication, June 5, 2016)

This political power is not limited to Rwanda and Uganda. A reporter at *The Nairobian*, a weekly English-language (tabloid) newspaper published by The Standard Group in Kenya, spoke about the influence of political leaders across the continent:

> Once they're in power, they control the instruments of power, unlike in developed countries where you have to stick to what the constitution says.

In Africa you know very well once you're sent into power you become more powerful even than the constitution itself. So I cannot guarantee we will have that freedom, it will hinge on the kind of president we will have. (Journalist 17, personal communication, February 28, 2019)

However, despite what may be seen as fewer political changes in Uganda and Rwanda, journalists in these countries still experience ups and downs in media freedoms dependent upon the political environment of the time. As discussed in Chapter 3, a reporter from the *Daily Monitor* in Uganda explained the lessening press freedom environment (and other "incredible losses to institutions") as a result of President Museveni's time in office:

I think the [press freedom] space is reducing. It's shrinking . . . it's a trend that is common with regimes that have overstayed their welcome. [Museveni] could easily do 40 years [in office]. He's almost unstoppable . . . for a system to achieve that, you achieve that with incredible losses to institutions. So, the judiciary has, over the years, been watered down. You have more compliant judges. You have judges appointed more on the basis of either they are optimistic or their political views being friendly to the establish-ment . . . the same with parliament. . . . But that's by design, because a weak parliament serves the interest of a dictatorship. And I consider about al-most every other institution of the state [to be similarly watered down]. So, naturally the media, even when it plays in the private sector space, cannot be spared. It follows therefore that media freedom can only keep shrinking, and there are motives to co-opt more journalists and shut down critical voices, either by giving them job offers—so you'll find a good number of very brilliant and objective journalists who were once critical of the govern-ment are now working for the president, working for parliament, working for an institution as a spokesperson, and whatnot. So you have a systematic attempt at co-opting journalists, so that you have less critical voices. And that certainly has taken a toll on not just press freedom, but also how much critical journalism we can have in the country. (Journalist 4, personal com-munication, June 5, 2018)

Thus, what is also clear from journalists in this book and from pre-vious work is that the development and regression of these spheres—democratization and backsliding, and the accompanying press freedom and press censorship—is not linear. Despite Kenya currently being home to more press freedom than neighbouring countries, the reporter at *The Nairobian* warned that such a standing is not guaranteed:

> In the future I don't know the kind of president we might have, we might end up having a dictator. And if we have a dictator then the press freedom will not be guaranteed. So it will depend. Remember I told you we are still, we've not developed. So we cannot predict that in [the] future we will have a vibrant press, I will be lying because we'll end up having a dictator like in other countries, our neighbours, there'll be no freedom. (Journalist 17, personal communication, February 28, 2019)

In addition to the length and scope of a political leader's tenure, journalists in these East African nations spoke about other political-related events and structures, specifically post-election violence and politician-owned media houses, that they perceive as particularly impactful to press freedom.

Elections and Their Aftermath

Building from the journalists' discussions about the impacts of political leaders remaining in power for extended periods of time, it is well documented that competitive multiparty elections are a key component of a democracy (see, e.g., Adejumobi, 2000; Harbeson & Rothchild, 2009), but they don't always equal democracy. Kenya, for example, "holds free and regular elections, [but] political elites regularly intimidate political opposition as well as journalists and the judiciary" (Yoxon, 2017, para. 7). Such election malpractice can lead the public and the opposition to protest the structure or results of the election, which can move leaders, particularly authoritarian leaders, to resort to violence in an effort to end the dissent (Hafner-Burton et al., 2014; Tucker, 2007). And those efforts to end dissent often include goals of suppressing the news media (Gandhi & Lust-Okar, 2009) and preventing access to the internet (Odhiambo, 2017). Walulya and Nassanga (2020) found that Ugandan journalists faced increased safety risks during elections, with much of the violence coming from state security forces. In South Africa in 2016, the public broadcaster, the South African Broadcasting Corporation, censored coverage of violent protests in the run-up to local elections and fired journalists who protested the limited coverage (Abramowitz, 2017).

In addition to violence leading up to and during an election, in the case of Kenya, journalists spoke about the public and political reactions, as well as actions of journalists and media houses *following* elections, as being an important consideration when examining levels of press freedom. As was discussed in Chapter 4, Kenya has experienced notable post-election violence, which has led to restrictions imposed on the press, some of which are short-lived and others of which linger and seep into government ideologies and policies regulating the media. Using post-election violence as an excuse to suppress the media is not unique to Kenya. Journalists experienced violence and censorship during post-election protests in Mongolia (Reporters Without Borders, 2008) and before and after 2016 general elections in Zambia (Abramowitz, 2017), and journalists and media outlets had their credentials removed during and after the 2016 United States election of Donald Trump (Gimson, 2017), among many other examples, making it important to consider pre- and post-election violence and any accompanying (short- and long-term) media restrictions.

Taking a different avenue but with similar results, in Rwanda, elections reinforce existing media restrictions and ecosystems, as journalists are not able to report on any opposition candidates or movements—and those who do usually disappear or flee the country (Fox, 2019; Jalloh, 2021). The restrictions may come before, during, or after an election and/or they may be long-held government positions or temporary restrictions, but might be linked to the relationship that political, business, and tribal leaders have with media houses.

Media Ownership

Scholars have suggested that a part of political systems in many sub-Saharan African nations is ethno-patrimonialism, where class divisions have not fully materialized due to underdevelopment, and, thus, ethnic and regional associations form significant parts of collective identities (Bratton & van de Walle, 1994). In Kenya, media houses are often owned by members of distinct tribes who use their political ideologies to influence coverage, as discussed in Chapter 4. Ambala (2016) referred to this as "'tribal' hegemony in media ownership" (p. 59); those media owners are often using their newspaper to pursue their own political or economic interests (Nyanjom, 2012). While this is not unique to Kenya (it has been well documented in Cameroon and other nations [Nyamnjoh, 2005]), this ownership structure, and accompanying ideological and journalistic bent, contributed to the post-election violence in Kenya, and journalists in all three countries spoke about the strong impact that politician-owned or tribe-specific media houses have on press freedom in their countries.

This impact can be direct censorship, as described in the previous chapters, but it can also be more subtle. A reporter at the *Daily Nation* in Kenya explained the complexities of political ownership: "For example, the Standard Group, KTN and all that, the tribe—the former president is the owner and his son. So you are most likely to see members from his ethnic group . . . at the top of the editorial, the top of the management of the company" (Journalist 14, personal communication, February 27, 2019).

Similar to what occurred during the post-election violence in Kenya but on a smaller scale, in Uganda in 2012 a government-run radio station, Voice of Bundibugyo, reportedly fired employees for "promoting tribal clashes," although it is unclear whether those staff members were fired for being members of an opposing tribe (Kabuju, 2012, p. 1). And, as was discussed at length in Chapters 1 and 2, news media—radio, in particular—were used to promote specific extremist ideologies and perpetuate violence in Rwanda leading up to and during the genocide against the Tutsi.

These tribal/political ownership structures deeply impact the work that journalists can do, according to study participants. Our interviews with journalists revealed that press freedom fluctuates based on who owns each media house, as well as how connected that owner and their party or tribe is to the political leadership at local and national levels. As mentioned in Chapter 4, the revise editor at *People Daily* in Kenya explained how journalists may stop pursuing a story when they learn that they are investigating a source who is connected to their boss, who is a politician (Journalist 13, personal communication, February 27, 2019). Similarly in Uganda, a reporter from Uganda Radio Network explained that media ownership is a problem from politicians as well as businessmen who are only interested in profits and not the rights of their journalists:

> What's happening is that 90% of the media houses in this country [are] owned by politicians. And these are politicians who were leaning towards the government. And the other percentage is owned by businessmen who are looking at profit. So, they're not really fighting for us. (Journalist 17, personal communication, June 7, 2018)

In Rwanda, where government control over the media is particularly strong, journalists also spoke about how the government's ownership of media houses limits topics that can be covered. A Rwanda-based news editor from *The East African* said:

> We don't have many people, like journalists, who can talk about those issues [human rights or criticism of the government], and you cannot say *The East African* is going to talk about those issues alone. So, like, maybe the international media can write stories, but local media cannot write such issues because the fear number one [is] that if we write maybe a story that "police is doing this," [or] "government is doing this," we are not going to get adverts, and if we don't get adverts, we are not going to survive. And also remember most of the media houses in Rwanda are owned by the state, so you can see that the state is not going to allow such stories to come up. (Journalist 18, personal communication, June 1, 2016)

A journalist who serves as an editor, reporter, and presenter at Radio Isango Star in Rwanda explained that even private/commercial media houses are deeply connected to the government and are thus limited in what they can report. This journalist said that they cannot report negatively about advertisers for financial reasons:

> We cannot do it [report critically about advertisers]. . . . We work for a commercial radio station, but when you look at our clients or people who give us adverts, they are either government institutions or those private companies, especially telecommunication companies. . . . We are too much relying on the government and such kind of people, so it is influencing our content. (Journalist 6, personal communication, May 29, 2016)

Similarly, an editor at the Kinyarwanda-language paper *Umusingi* in Rwanda spoke about the government refusing to purchase ads in private newspapers, essentially putting the paper out of business due to the country's media relying so heavily on government-funded advertising: "When you go to some government institutions, they tell you 'no we cannot advertise with your newspapers.' They advertise with *The New Times* [regarded as a government-run media house]. . . . We have a serious problem as if we are, like, blocked completely" (Journalist 9, personal communication, May 29, 2016).

However, Voltmer (2013) challenges the notion that commercial media houses are "the best guarantor for political independence," saying:

> Instead, the situation in many new democracies—and not only new ones, it has to be said—shows that the joint interests of political and economic

elites frequently hijack the media to pursue their own interests by control-
ling the range of issues that can be covered by the media. (p. 164)

So while political and tribal influences on media ownership can be problematic, so too can commercial interests be, with purely profit-seeking actors
bringing their own agendas.

In sum, the political environment, specifically who is in power and for
how long, the ways that leaders and citizens act during and after elections,
and political and tribal influences in media ownership all contribute to the
growing and shrinking spaces for media freedom and ought to be considered
when theorizing about global media systems.

Interpretation and Enforcement of Laws

Working in conjunction with media ownership are the policies that government officials create. Laws obviously impact the ways journalists do their
jobs, whether those lessen media freedoms by restricting access to people or
events, limit critical reporting, and so forth, or improve media freedoms by
legalizing access to information, removing or shortening punishments, etc.
Alongside the existence of these laws, data from this study suggest that the
ways in which those various laws are interpreted and enforced arguably play
an equally important role.

Chapter 2 highlighted the vaguely worded laws in Rwanda surrounding
genocide denial and divisionism that are used in wide-reaching ways to limit
the content that journalists can write about. A former journalist in Rwanda
who asked us to withhold their employer's name made it clear that journalists
would "never" publish something that could potentially "lead to" a charge
of genocide denial—they explained that they would not push the limits on
what is safe to write about, as it isn't always clear where the boundaries are
(Journalist 5, personal communication, May 28, 2016). Similarly, Ugandan
journalists spoke of vaguely worded libel and defamation laws which are
commonly levied against journalists or media houses that publish content
critical of President Museveni and his administration.

The vaguely worded nature and widespread use of these laws as censorship mechanisms can be thought of as unfair enforcement, which is similar
to how some journalists spoke of unequal enforcement of laws, particularly
for politicians. A Committee to Protect Journalists (2015) report on lawsuits
and restrictive legislation targeting journalists stated that "the mere threat of
punitive action and the uncertainty surrounding the laws' implementation

is enough to make journalists pause before airing or publishing sensitive stories" (para. 3). An associate editor at *Nairobi Business Monthly* in Kenya explained that even when laws exist, politicians find ways to work around them: "There's even a law [that] prohibit[s] them [politicians] from owning a [media house]—yeah probably there is . . . [but] they circumvent it, 'I'll own it through my son, I'll own it through a partner'" (Journalist 27, personal communication, March 6, 2019). Further, other scholars have noted that regulations are unevenly distributed among media houses (Odongo, 2014) due to the owners of some media house maintaining strong political and financial power, resulting in a system where government regulators look the other way and "handle commercial media owners with kid gloves" (Chibita, 2009, p. 303).

In addition to changing political climates, problems after elections, and unfair litigious efforts, journalists spoke about a number of other factors that contribute to the depth of each country's mediascape (and interweave with why the political domain is the way that it is). One element commonly discussed is the connections that a city, country, or leader has to other nations.

International Linkages

Interviews revealed a belief among journalists in Kenya that strategic actions taken by the government to establish links with Western countries have resulted in substantial improvements in the country's press freedom landscape. However, with democratic backsliding occurring in some Western nations and China's growing influence in Africa and on African media systems, certain links may not always promote democracy and may introduce competing ideologies.

Chapter 4 highlighted the notable international linkages that Kenyan government officials have, particularly with Western governments and organizations, and how those contribute to a more free media environment. However, it is not just Kenyan officials that understand the importance of these global connections. As discussed in Chapter 2, President Kagame of Rwanda has positive relationships with leaders of many Western nations (hence his nickname, the "darling tyrant"). He has undertaken intentional efforts to build, maintain, and showcase these relationships (Sobel Cohen & McIntyre, 2021), and the country has seen substantial and sustained economic growth (Sundaram, 2014, para. 1; World Bank, 2020a). In recent years the country has taken concrete steps to make itself more attractive to foreign tourists and businesses. In 2020 and 2021, the Rwandan government implemented substantial policy reforms designed to, among other things, increase foreign direct investment and attract foreign companies to operate in the newly created Kigali International Financial Centre (U.S. Department of State, 2021). Another component of this progress in Rwanda is in the tourism industry, which has seen rapid growth in recent years (Adekoya, 2020). Much of this can be attributed to a nation branding campaign undertaken by the government of Rwanda, which has, among other things, included a $40 million USD sponsorship of Arsenal FC (a decision that drew criticism: "Paul Kagame leaves his country to give astronomical sums to Arsenal when Rwandan orphans are so poor that they cannot afford a ball to play football" [Adekoya, 2020, para. 18]). Uganda has similarly undertaken nation branding efforts to increase tourism, most recently launching a new campaign, "Explore Uganda," in early 2022 (Edwin, 2022). However, these efforts are still in their infancy in Rwanda, and slightly older in Uganda, but have not yet established the deep ties (and financial investments) that Kenya has with international partners.

However, like other elements discussed in this chapter, these international linkages fluctuate given global geopolitical changes and can cause press freedom levels to reactively fluctuate. If you recall from Chapter 4, the revise editor at *People Daily* in Nairobi explained that as the political and press freedom environment in the United States changed under President Donald Trump, resulting in a lack of support for media freedom also in Kenya and across Africa, a space was created for China to fill with its oppressive media practices. China's growing links across the continent cannot be ignored, as they are already influencing African media ecosystems and have the potential to do so more strongly in the future.

Chapter 4 discussed ways in which Kenyan journalists were pushing back on China's editorial influence, and recent research reveals that news organizations in 30 African nations used less wire content from Xinhua compared to other global news organizations, such as Reuters and AFP (Madrid-Morales, 2021). This may suggest that while the Chinese presence in Africa and on African mediascapes existed in the past and is growing—and may change East Africa's geopolitical positions in the future—linkages with Western countries remain strong (likely due to and dating back to colonization and the ongoing monopolization of global news agencies in the global north and accompanying unidirectional flow of information that decades of scholars have documented (e.g., Boyd-Barrett, 1980; Paterson, 2011). However, the pushback seen from Kenyan journalists, specifically, may be due to their experiences with a relatively free press as well as operating within an increasingly vibrant civil society.

Growth of a Vibrant Civil Society

Another element that journalists said influences development and democratization, and in turn improves and lessens levels of press freedom, is the growth (or silencing) of a dynamic civil society. Ranging from the presence (or absence) and reach of nongovernmental organizations (NGOs), to the social norms of societies, to journalism cultures in each of these countries, journalists discussed a number of factors that result in fluctuating levels of empowerment of civil society, which then impact media freedoms. The deputy news editor at *People Daily* in Kenya spoke broadly about civil society, saying:

> We have a very vibrant civil society, maybe that's one thing you can say that makes sure that every time the government oversteps boundaries, it's there to say 'No, I think this is wrong.' So for us, I think the civil society is one of the institutions that makes sure our [media] freedom is protected. (Journalist 10, personal communication, February 27, 2019)

More specifically, journalists spoke about elements of a vibrant civil society including: the role that nongovernmental organizations play, the personality of citizens and social expectations regarding self-expression, and the culture surrounding journalism in each country.

Nongovernmental Organizations

Interwoven with previous discussions about a nation's links to other countries is the point made by journalists that the presence of NGOs in a country, and their ability (or lack thereof) to do impactful work, contributes to the strength of that country's civil society, which can directly impact media freedoms. Chapter 4 highlighted the ways in which an array of international linkages led journalists to view Kenya as a leader in the region. In addition to the location, treaties, relationships, and ideologies discussed in Chapter 4, organizations, particularly nongovernmental, are important players in shaping civil society and resulting media ecosystems.

A reporter at *Business Daily* in Kenya explained that the growth of NGOs headquartered in and around Nairobi has led to increased press freedom levels by "driv[ing] certain agendas" or ideologies that promote journalists rights:

> [International NGOs based in Kenya] really helped to drive certain agendas that no one else would try to fund or even to work on. I remember I used to cover murder[s] committed, especially committed by the police, and you would not get anybody to talk about them. But an NGO called the Independent Medico Legal Unit and then the Kenya Human Rights Commission who hired doctors to conduct post-mortems and prepare pathologists' reports and release it and point fingers [would talk]; no one else would. So I think also allowing these NGOs to come [to Kenya] and highlight some of these issues really helped create more room for freedom to thrive. (Journalist 9, personal communication, February 27, 2019)

What is important to note here is that those organizations that the *Business Daily* reporter mentioned are NGOs, compared to government bodies, which were commonly mentioned by Rwandan journalists as shaping public and policy perspectives surrounding the media. For example, the former Media High Council was commonly mentioned by journalists in Rwanda as shaping their work as well as public and policy ideologies regarding the press. The Council was a regulatory body that, at times, censored and shut down news organizations (Reporters Without Borders, 2010). It was dismantled in 2021 and responsibilities were distributed among other government bodies, particularly the Rwandan Ministry of Local Government and the Rwanda Governance Board (IGIHE, 2021). Global press freedom NGOs regularly speak out in support of journalists in Rwanda, but critics point out the difficulty of an organization of any kind operating in the country due to tight government control:

> In the context of tech companies operating in Rwanda, "The Rwandan government has a history of censoring websites, media organizations and individuals, including journalists. A branch of government is specifically designated to launch cyberattacks both within and outside the country for the sake of national security. That has likely kept some of the biggest players

away from the country, despite its tech-friendly policies and sweeping infrastructure." If American corporations opened up data centers or started offering local services . . . they would then be subject to the government's whims as well. "If you are not comfortable fulfilling government requests because of human rights issues in a country, you should not put servers or employees there. . . . You should stay the hell out of the country . . . so you don't necessarily have any kind of obligation to fulfill its legal requests." (Lang, 2018, para. 27–30)

Such concerns about working in Rwanda undoubtedly extend to NGOs, particularly those working on issues at odds with the government's agenda. The absence of such organizations leads to a less powerful civil society.

Social Norms
Journalists spoke about the personalities of individuals and publics and broader social norms as contributing to the development of a free media space. Many journalists in Kenya expressed the belief that the personality of Kenyans and the social expectations surrounding speaking in public played a part in helping the country democratize and grow and maintain press freedoms. A Kenya-based BBC reporter and news anchor explained that they believe character traits of Kenyans have helped the nation get to a different position than its neighbours:

> Kenyans are considered to be the most aggressive people in East Africa so it's easier for us to go on the streets and advocate for an end to dictatorship or advocate for more rights to the judiciary or advocate for an independent judiciary. It might not work for Uganda—Uganda is a military dictatorship. At least the Kenyan president is a civilian, he comes from a civilian background. We've never had a military dictatorship in Kenya so we cannot relate to the barrel of the gun because we don't know it, but beyond that I also think [there] is a factor that works for us—that the Kenyan people are, on average, more educated or more aware of happenings globally than the other East Africans. (Journalist 32, personal communication, March 8, 2019)

Similarly, an associate editor at *Nairobi Business Monthly* in Kenya said, "It's just the personality of the people—we don't sit back, we go to the street even though our opposition leader joined hands with the government . . . we press on and we ask for these rights" (Journalist 27, personal communication, March 2, 2019).

On the other end of the spectrum, scholars have noted relevant findings about differences in social customs surrounding self-expression in Rwanda, for unique reasons. Sommers (2012) argued that young men in Rwanda are "stuck" in adolescence due to government actions that stack the odds against them. In Rwanda, Grant (2015) found a distrust between friends and family members (referred to as a "quiet insecurity") as a result of heavy state control under the name of security and unity that lead Rwandans to avoid discussing sensitive topics such as politics or ethnicity (though Grant [2015] ultimately concluded that the complicated web of ways that youth navigate Rwandan Patriotic Front controls ultimately gives them a "quiet agency"—for example, writing a song with controversial lyrics but not allowing many people to ever hear the song). Silence is an expected mode of dealing with hardship in the country (Burnet, 2012), and many Rwandans view it as morally right to avoid making too much of your own problems so as to not burden others with them (Eramian, 2017). In fact, there exists a social expectation in the country that people conceal many of their own thoughts and feelings (Ingelaere, 2018), a cultural norm of "sharing in the unsaid" (de Lame, 2013, p. 294).

Interestingly, personality traits or cultural norms surrounding communication did not come up during interviews with Ugandan journalists, whereas it stood out in conversations in Rwanda and Kenya. A Nairobi-based digital reporter for CNN speculated about the situation in Uganda, saying:

> I think about the society, like where one comes from. Uganda, for example, is a more what would I say, submissive, society. Like, I think both male and female, they're more submissive . . . but it all starts with the leaders—if the people can't speak freely about Museveni, about the regime, then it goes down to the people, so they will also not feel free to speak against the issues . . . even the issues like human rights issues, justice issues. (Journalist 29, personal communication, March 6, 2019)

However, that was just the perspective of one interviewee, and the absence of this topic in discussions in Uganda reinforces the point that personality appears to play a notable role in Kenya and Rwanda, where it lies on opposite ends of the spectrum (bold and talkative versus quiet and secretive), and Uganda likely sits in the middle.

The Kenyan cultural norm—or personality trait, as some interviewees referred to it—more closely resembles that of Western nations, which often value individualism and self-expression. While the Rwandan social tradition could be viewed as less beneficial to the fight for human rights, it also rests upon notions of survival, sensitivity, and empathy given their past. And this discussion of personality traits can present a chicken-and-egg scenario: Kenyans have the ability to speak freely, so they do; Rwandans can be severely punished for speaking critically (though, given their past, they may not yet want to), so they don't. Whether Rwandans are "stuck" or have their own unique (quiet) agency, they do not have the ability to speak out or take to the streets in the way(s) that journalists spoke about Kenyans doing.

Journalism Culture

In addition to influences by leaders and members of the general public, our findings also reveal an important role that journalists themselves, and the subsequently fostered journalism culture, play in the promotion of press freedom. Journalists spoke about the ways in which the strength of journalism as a profession (pay, ethical behaviour, amount of training, strength of professional organizations, etc.) contributes to media freedom levels in each country.

When asked about the challenges that they face, 95.1% of the journalists we surveyed noted that low pay was a challenge, followed by 80% of respondents who noted a lack of the necessary equipment and 80% who identified economic issues such as a lack of advertising revenue. Interviews confirmed that finance-related challenges were present in all three countries. The deputy news editor at *People Daily* in Kenya said:

> Many news organizations are also dependent on advertising from commercial companies. That means they have to play ball in order to get advertisement. And then that means that sometimes you have to sort of self-censor yourself so that you don't get into the bad side of who you're advertising for. In the same light, the government in terms of advertising, it has centralized advertising under the government agency, it's called GAA [Government Advertising Agency], which means that all government adverts go through that one agency . . . that's one way the government uses to muscle. . . . If you say anything bad about the government then advertising will not come

your way and government being the biggest advertiser, it means that you will be out of business if you don't listen to what the government tells you. (Journalist 10, personal communication, February 27, 2019)

In addition to advertising revenue, journalists in all three countries noted a lack of professional training opportunities. A former reporter who works with the Uganda Hub for Investigative Media in Uganda spoke about journalist pay issues in relation to a lack of training:

Why are journalists not sufficiently trained? You know, journalism is one profession that is easy to get it. . . . If I have a good voice I can just walk in there, in the radio station, in a certain radio station, and I'll become a journalist. I'll go on air, start repeating news. Thereafter, I'll start speaking interviews from different people where I have zero idea about—and this is actually more to do with media houses themselves because most of the media houses don't have serious keys to train. . . . Media houses actually have a problem of paying—of remunerating journalists. . . . There's a lot of work that's needed to the investment of human resource within the media houses. No media house has a well-established scheme for training journalists. . . . Some journalists who have their personal initiative to apply for training schemes, like, for, even here or even outside the country, but media houses don't have that. That's why it is hard for any media house in Uganda now to keep good journalists. . . .They can't live on the pay, the salaries of media houses. (Journalist 18, personal communication, June 7, 2018)

For any individual or organization, being in financial trouble can lead to a temptation for unethical behaviour, and such is the case in the journalism industry in the region, according to study findings. A journalist in a management role at *The East African* in Uganda said:

One of the biggest challenges I would think is we have poorly paid, poorly trained journalists. If people are poorly paid, they're likely to be easily influenced by politicians, by state security operatives because they're giving them a little bit more money. If people are poorly trained, they will not know what exactly is their responsibility. (Journalist 27, personal communication, June 12, 2018)

Journalists in Uganda and Kenya spoke about this lack of pay and lack of training resulting in a culture of bribery. Additionally, as discussed in Chapter 3, in Uganda, the lack of pay and culture of bribery have resulted in spies in the newsroom, according to journalists (McIntyre & Sobel Cohen, 2021b).

Across the three nations, 36.8% of respondents agreed or strongly agreed with the statement "Journalists in my country act in a professional manner"; 30.5% agreed or strongly agreed with the statement "Journalists in my country have access to many training opportunities"; and 44.1% said most reporters in their country have formal journalism training (studied journalism at university, completed a certificate program, etc.). Interestingly, 36.4% of survey respondents agreed or strongly agreed that journalists in their country act ethically, however 36.1% of respondents also agreed or strongly agreed that journalists in their country regularly accept bribes. However, Table 5.1 shows noteworthy between-country differences.

Fewer survey respondents in Rwanda agreed or strongly agreed that journalists in their country act in a professional manner, compared to respondents in Uganda and Kenya. However, journalists in Rwanda more commonly agreed that reporters in their country have access to many training opportunities, and more commonly reported that, in general, journalists

Table 5.1 Percentages of Survey Respondents in Each Country That Agreed or Strongly Agreed with Each Statement

	Rwanda	Uganda	Kenya
Journalists in my country act in a professional manner	38.1% ($n = 48$)	48.9% ($n = 64$)	50.6% ($n = 44$)
Journalists in my country have access to many training opportunities	51.7% ($n = 63$)	28.1% ($n = 36$)	34.4% ($n = 30$)
Most reporters in my country have formal training in journalism (studied in uni)	47.2% ($n = 60$)	46.6% ($n = 60$)	77.0% ($n = 67$)
Journalists in my country regularly accept bribes	36.4% ($n = 44$)	48.9% ($n = 63$)	54.7% ($n = 47$)
In general, journalists in my country act ethically	47.2% ($n = 59$)	45.3% ($n = 58$)	43.0% ($n = 37$)

Note. The total number of people who answered these questions in Rwanda ranged from 121 to 127, in Uganda 128 to 131, and in Kenya 86 to 87.

in their country act ethically; in addition, fewer respondents agreed that journalists in the country regularly accept bribes. Respondents from Kenya overwhelmingly agreed that most reporters in their country have formal journalism training (which would make sense, given the higher number of journalism schools in the country); however, these same respondents also noted the highest percentage of agreement that their fellow journalists regularly accept bribes and reported the lowest agreement that, in general, journalists in the country act ethically. It could be argued that despite the presence of formal journalism training, the freedom that Kenyan journalists have is a double-edged sword—they have the ability to write about a wider range of topics, and report more critically, so they are more susceptible to bribes and other unethical behaviour. Journalists in Rwanda, on the other hand, are less inclined to accept bribes because they don't have the ability to write critically, thus, people in power wouldn't need to bribe a journalist to stop investigating them, for example.

While these financial challenges are certainly not unique to the East Africa region, they can create cracks in the strength of the journalism profession. Journalists also commonly spoke about the impacts of a lack of a unified professional journalism organization, both on the industry and on press freedom levels. For example, in Uganda, the reporter from Uganda Radio Network said:

> We do not have any journalist association that's worth its name in this country. The Ugandan Journalists Association is quite weak because all the leaders have been bribed by governments. So, we need a very strong journalist association that can stand up to government. (Journalist 17, personal communication, June 7, 2018)

Similarly, a reporter from the commercial television network NBS in Uganda said:

> The other affront to press freedom is that there's no association that can qualifiably [sic] relate [unify] all journalists in the country. So, while we have journalist associations, they don't have the right membership to be able to make demands. Yes, so many of the demands come through media owners and that is, of course, tricky because it goes back to the business arm. . . . So in the absence of a united journalists association, press freedom really lies in the hands of media owners and the state. (Journalist 3, personal communication, June 4, 2018)

While reporters may not think there exists a strong journalists association, a chief news editor at the government-run Kenya Broadcasting Corporation (KBC) in Kenya said that an editors collective is working on it:

> I'm a member of the Kenya Editors Guild and basically we are an organization of quite a number of editors from media houses in Kenya . . . [and] part of our engagement has been to push for press freedom to ensure that media is allowed space to operate as it should be. (Journalist 26, personal communication, March 5, 2019)

When asked about the challenges that they face and who holds responsibility for lessening those challenges—which can speak to the strength of journalism as a profession and the amount of agency that journalists feel they hold—journalists in the three nations pointed most strongly to the government as being to blame for many of their professional challenges: 62.2% of respondents agreed or strongly agreed that the government of their country was to blame for many of the challenges, compared to 25.6% of respondents who agreed or strongly agreed that individual journalists were to blame, and 54.2% who agreed or strongly agreed that media management (editors, publishers, etc.) were responsible for many of the industry's challenges. This could point to a strong journalistic culture in these countries and the region. Less than a quarter (22.8%) of respondents disagreed or strongly disagreed with the statement that the challenges that journalists face are mostly out of their control—which can suggest some degree of agency felt by journalists. Relatedly, 68.1% of respondents agreed or strongly agreed that they can do something to reduce the number of challenges that journalists face, which was also seen in interviews, particularly with journalists in Uganda.

An anchor/reporter at Urban TV in Uganda elaborated on the notion that journalists themselves hold some responsibility due to unethical behaviour:

> Many times, we have abused the freedom that we have as journalists. We've worked in the pockets of politicians, because again, we weren't passionate about journalism. We just wanted to pass exams, get a career, work, and [then ended up saying], "Oh, there is not enough money in here. But, hey, there is that politician who wants to get [in] office. He has a propaganda story to tell. I will work up through his pockets." You know? And being bankrolled to tell a story. . . . Many times, we have PR people in the newsrooms and they are reporting for their interests in the field because this supplements their salaries well enough. And if we get to be castigated

enough, and we need something to fall back to, press freedom sounds like something good. We *are* being abused, you know, with our press freedom. But that said, inasmuch as we, sometimes, bring this to ourselves. (Journalist 11, personal communication, June 6, 2018)

Similarly, a journalist at the commercial online magazine Eagle Online in Uganda said:

If we were organized and we have one strong association as journalists, then we would even question ourselves and see who the hell is there doing that [unethical reporting and/or accepting bribes] in the village. You know, we'll even go there to question whatever they're doing. . . . And so, we contribute 80% of the lack of press freedom as journalists. (Journalist 9, personal communication, June 6, 2018)

Summary

In sum, a number of cross-border similarities and differences emerged from this research which point to specific factors that can move forward press freedom environments as well as push them backward and which should be considered when theorizing about and/or classifying global media systems. Distance from conflict, political benchmarks (specifically who is in office and for how long, elections and their aftermath, and political and tribal influences on media ownership), international linkages, and the vibrancy of civil society (including nongovernmental organizations, social norms, and journalism cultures) are some examples—though not an exhaustive list—of criteria that activists, scholars, media practitioners, and diplomats can consider when aiming to understand how and why national and regional media systems function in the ways that they do.

Note

1. It is important to note that while some journalists in Rwanda and Uganda spoke about the need for political change, many of these individuals, particularly in Rwanda, are severely restricted from speaking in such a way—and those who did, did so under the potential for significant personal and professional consequences.

6

Conclusion

A Call for New Considerations in Understanding Press Freedom

Via in-depth examinations of the media systems in Rwanda, Uganda, and Kenya, new understandings emerged about how free the press is in each of these three nations, by what measures, and with what implications for development and democratization. Journalists in all three countries reported wanting enhanced media freedoms beyond what they currently have, but many complexities exist regarding what their current and desired media landscapes look like.

Summary of Press Freedom—and Its Complexities—in Each Country

In Rwanda, the 1994 genocide against the Tutsi still permeates many aspects of society, including the media landscape. The amount of press freedom in the country, as well as boundaries and definitions of media freedom, are perceived differently by outsiders than by those within Rwanda. Outsiders—primarily press freedom NGOs, scholars, and foreign journalists—have documented intense government control over media content via wide-reaching laws, withholding advertising revenue, harassment, detention and killing of journalists, the shutting down of domestic and international media outlets, and an intentionally fostered culture of silence (Amah, 2018; Committee to Protect Journalists, 2022; Freedom House, 2022a; Frère, 2009; Reporters Without Borders, 2022c; Sundaram, 2016). On the other hand, insiders claim that outsiders do not understand the role of media in the country, given its history and unique complexities. In interviews with us, Rwandan journalists said they felt they had more freedom than international rankings reflect and significantly more freedom than they had 25 years

Press Freedom and the (Crooked) Path Toward Democracy. Meghan Sobel Cohen and Karen McIntyre Hopkinson,
Oxford University Press. © Oxford University Press 2023. DOI: 10.1093/oso/9780197634202.003.0006

ago. Regarding the severe limits on press freedom that outsiders claim they experience, journalists in Rwanda described a desire to self-censor in order to promote development, maintain peace, and right the wrongs of their predecessors during the genocide. Journalists in Rwanda also reported feeling as if they are free because they know how to report things in ways that work around government restrictions. At times, what the journalists described as media freedom simultaneously sounded like what many outside Rwanda would consider restrictions. For example, journalists would say they are free but then explain the topics they could not cover. This contradiction would befit a situation of government media censorship as well as government control of ideologies and narratives, as the Rwandan journalist that was in a management role at Great Lakes Voice (Journalist 23, personal communication, June 5, 2016) described in Chapter 5. This makes it clear that the perceptions of local journalists coupled with understandings of history and present-day context are crucial in understanding the complexities of press freedom in different countries, particularly those with non-democratic governments.

While journalists in Uganda and Kenya have more press freedom than do journalists in Rwanda, the road to that freedom (and with that freedom) has not been straightforward. Journalists in Uganda agree with international press freedom rankings pointing to restrictions, but they perceive their freedoms to be lessening, despite some outside of Uganda pointing to a vibrant media environment due to a large number of media houses and some legal rulings in favor of the media (Freedom House, 2022b). Journalists that we spoke to, as well as other scholars, have documented a long history of press suppression in Uganda as well as ongoing and sustained censorship, harassment, and violence against journalists (Chibita & Fourie, 2007; Freedom House, 2022b; Isoba, 1980; Kalyango & Eckler, 2010; Mwesige, 2004). Journalists talked to us a great deal about the declining amount of press freedom they are experiencing as President Museveni continues to hold onto his presidential seat, despite an otherwise largely peaceful time in the country. Journalists reported feeling discouraged and demoralized, which, along with low pay and a lack of training opportunities, has created a system where bribes and newsroom spies are commonplace. Ugandan journalists spoke about some of the responsibility that they hold in creating the current press freedom environment due to many journalists "work[ing] in the pockets of politicians," as an anchor/reporter at Urban TV in Uganda (Journalist 11, personal communication, June 6, 2018) put it, and while they overall agree with global press freedom rankings, their path to today's media landscape has been crooked and appears to be moving in the wrong direction.

In Kenya, like Rwanda, many journalists felt that they had more freedom than international ratings indicated, but even in a country where political leadership changes, press freedom ebbs and flows in reaction to who the current leader is, spurts of political violence, influences on ownership, political and economic connections to other countries, and general ideology and culture. Kenyan journalists have an optimistic outlook on press freedom in the future but acknowledge that the president plays a key role, and therefore, increasing freedom is not guaranteed down the road, especially as concerns linger about post-election violence and related ideological influences. Fortunately, Kenya's international connections, vibrant civil society, and culture of public conversation and debate create a strong backdrop for continued support for media freedom.

There is growing recognition that while media can play a role in escalating conflict, as we saw in the genocide against the Tutsi in Rwanda and during post-election violence in Kenya, they can also play a role in peacebuilding and democratization. For example, Rwandan journalists view themselves as unifiers and understand one of their roles to be maintaining peace. Additionally, the majority of journalists surveyed in all three of the East African countries agreed or strongly agreed that news media in their country play a positive role in democratization. And this may be a result of, or the catalyst for, the public trusting media. Public trust in media is particularly strong in Kenya, and journalists think that the public has fought for them, which contributes to the high level of press freedom in the country. Public trust has enhanced complexities in Rwanda and Uganda, and while trust is higher in these countries than in many others around the world, there is not necessarily the same public support for press freedom in those countries as there is in Kenya.

Revisiting the Theories and Ranking Systems

While findings from this research lend support to previous work positioning Kenya's mediascape as the most free of the three countries, Uganda's in the middle, and Rwanda's as the most restrictive, what has (hopefully) become clear is that understanding these media environments—and classifying them, theoretically and practically—is more complicated than existing metrics may indicate. While journalists in each of these three countries may roughly define press freedom the same (reporting without interference), much debate exists regarding how much press freedom they have, in what capacity, whether they even want it, and what factors cause it to fluctuate. The media environments must be uniquely interpreted given each country's history and context and the fact that "both forces of [press] control and freedom are in a constant state of flux" (Ibelema et al., 2000, p. 112). Media ecosystems are not one-size-fits-all; thus, theories must account for forward progress, peacebuilding, and democracy-building, but also transitions, changes, backsliding, and hiccups. Further, ranking systems must account for histories and the ways in which journalism is constrained by structures and policies, and simultaneously how journalists manoeuvre through their constrained environments in innovative ways, creating their own journalistic practices and culture that may not ascribe to normative, often Western, practices.

This book does not intend to claim that existing theories and frameworks classifying media systems are invalid, but rather, that they may not be comprehensive enough and they are complicated by each country's unique factors. While it is possible that Kenya could be squeezed in, Rwanda and Uganda, for example, would not fit in any of Hallin and Mancini's (2004, 2012) proposed models of media systems (something that they and others openly admit). A number of factors contribute to these models not applying to the studied East African media systems given the unique aspects of postcolonial African communities, including ideologies about the importance of community, cultural norms due to historical events and processes, a lack of necessary technology and equipment, low pay and insufficient training, selfcensorship and a dependency on government advertising revenue, and loose interpretation and enforcement of laws.

Hachten's (1981, 1996) five normative concepts of the press (authoritarian, Western, Communist, revolutionary, and developmental), which he later revised to four dimensions after the fall of the Soviet Union (authoritarian, Western, revolutionary, and developmental), attempted to more accurately account for variations in the world's media systems. However, the reality of each country's history and political and press transitions make even these typologies difficult to accurately employ. For example, a nation having an authoritarian leader in power undoubtedly matters for press freedom, but that alone is not enough to understand the mediascape and fairly classify it. Both Rwanda and Uganda have authoritarian leaders in power and have for many years, but as described in Chapters 2 and 3, these two countries have notably different mediascapes; Rwanda is moving forward, with enhanced press freedom, and Uganda is backsliding with lessening freedoms and enhanced restrictions.

In a similar vein, media development theory argues that "social responsibility comes before media rights and freedoms" (McQuail, 2010, p. 151) and that while media freedoms are desirable, they come behind the need for political, economic, social, and cultural developments (McQuail, 1983, 2010). Data indicate that journalists in Rwanda may presently subscribe to this line of thinking, or are required to operate within this structure currently, but the other two countries may suggest that this doesn't hold in the long term. It is possible that media development theory can be a short-term explanation for why aspects of media systems function a certain way in the aftermath of conflict, but as you factor in distance from conflict this becomes less relevant. And further, scholars have noted that Rwanda "highlights some of the problems involved in a sequencing approach to democratizing the media, which puts stability and nation-building before other values, such as press freedom and an open expression of opinions in the public sphere" (He, 2001; Linz & Stepan, 1996, as cited in Voltmer, 2013, p. 193).

Nisbet and Moehler's (2005) five models—open democratic, liberalized democratic, liberalized autocratic, closed autocratic, and repressive autocratic—were designed to apply to developing nations and thus allow for greater applicability than previously developed classification systems. However, as earlier chapters showcased, while the political systems in these countries may align with one of these models for a short or long period of time, the lived experiences of journalists are more complicated and fluid than classification systems often allow. While these political demarcations are a good place to start when thinking about media systems operating outside of mature democracies, additional nuance and context is necessary. Utilizing these five models in conjunction with the elements discussed in Chapter 5 may allow for a more holistic look at press landscapes and their ever-changing complexities, accounting for the fact that the work that a journalist does may align with a country's political, social, and economic goals one day and be at odds with, or be shining a light on problems with, those very aims the next day. And even within political environments that stay the same for years or decades, transitions occur, complexities arise, violence starts, violence ends, ownership structures change, and so on.

A somewhat cyclical relationship exists where calls are put forth for more applicable theories of media systems beyond Western notions of the press, a framework or theory is put forward, and then that framework appears insufficient and calls are put forth for a new, more applicable, and, in Musa's (1997) word, "practicable" framework. Perhaps the reason that existing frameworks fail to hold applicability for extended periods of time is that the histories, contestations, and political changes, and accompanying social, cultural, and legal transformations of each nation fluctuate in unique ways that may allow a certain theory to apply in one moment in time but not another.

More broadly, much existing work tends to (consciously or not) operate on a presumption of linearity in that press freedom and democracy conjointly develop in a forward-moving progression (e.g., a country could be reclassified as it moves through the ranks of democratization: from repressive autocratic to closed autocratic to liberalized autocratic, for instance). Even without directly saying so, there is an implication that despite certain states of existence or specific moments in time, ultimately media systems progress alongside forward-moving democratization. This book spotlights the fluidity of political change that necessitates more historically informed views of media systems that do not fit into the confines of existing theories. Ultimately, press freedom means different things in different places and plays out in unique ways, making it difficult for any theory to aptly apply.

Similarly, in addition to theories lacking the necessary nuance and contextualization, so, too, do press freedom ranking systems. While ranking systems from organizations such as Reporters Without Borders and Freedom House provide a useful base of knowledge, similar to theory, they have flaws. As mentioned in Chapter 2, ranking indices have been criticized for unclear methods and conceptual bases, static nature, and Western biases (Becker et al., 2007; Fiedler & Frère, 2018; Schneider, 2014; Sobel & McIntyre, 2019). The reality is that press landscapes are more complicated than can be accounted for in such a structure. As discussed in earlier chapters, for example, journalists in Rwanda disagree with the country's rankings and journalists in Uganda agree with them. Context must be considered and one should not judge a country's level of press freedom solely by looking at its ranking.

Influencing Factors to Consider

The findings shared in this book about each country's mediascape, taken in conjunction with a review of prominent theoretical frameworks utilized in media studies and international communication fields, showcase how theory and rankings are helpful, but they don't always account for peculiarities. As such, this book can be taken as a call for scholars to reconsider the use and applicability of existing frameworks and to consider a specific set of factors to better understand media systems in a more historically and contextually informed manner. As described in Chapter 5, this book puts forward an array of factors that can help contextualize the uniqueness and complexity of each country's media environment. This is not an exhaustive list; instead, we hope these factors can be incorporated into existing frameworks and ranking systems to provide a starting place for deeper nuanced thinking about media systems outside the Western world. We hope the list of factors can continue to be built upon in the years to come.

First, journalists in these three East African nations, coupled with secondary literature, suggest that the distance a country or community is from conflict (in its many forms) plays an important role in how politics and the press interweave. In Rwanda, a positive relationship is seen between press freedom and distance from conflict, suggesting that the longer a nation experiences peace, the more press freedom the country will have. At first glance this relationship seems to hold when looking at other countries in the region, too; some of the conflict-related restrictions that Ugandan journalists faced have lessened as the country has moved further away from conflict, and Kenya has maintained relative peace for a longer period of time and, thus, has undeniably more press freedom than the other two countries of study. However, as deeper dives into the Kenyan and Ugandan mediascapes show, even though this positive relationship (longer period of peace leads to enhanced press freedom) generally holds, it is not always linear as points of intense censorship pop up and ideologies of control are maintained. As Chapter 3 highlighted, although Uganda has maintained peace in recent years, press freedom in the country is backsliding and the ideologies behind the restrictions (that government officials should not trust journalists and should not be forthcoming with information) remain. Thus, while distance from conflict can be a worthy indicator of some components of press freedom, it alone is not nuanced enough to determine the level of press freedom in a country.

Additional factors that journalists said influence media environments include political benchmarks (specifically, who is in office and for how long, what happens during elections and especially what happens in their aftermath, what political and tribal influences exist in media ownership, and how laws are interpreted and enforced), international linkages, and the strength of a country's civil society (including nongovernmental organizations, social norms, and journalism cultures).

The media-politics nexus is, of course, paramount when thinking about why media function in the way(s) that they do. Specifically, the amount of time that a president is in office has severe impacts on media systems, but it isn't always straightforward in that the longer a president is in office the less press freedom the nation receives; Rwandan journalists report increasing media freedoms as Kagame's tenure continues, but Ugandan journalists are experiencing the opposite, and in Kenya, despite having more media freedoms (and political transfers of power) than other nations in the region, journalists still experienced fluctuating media freedoms based on who was in office and for how long. In addition to the impacts of political leaders remaining in power for extended periods of time, considering the prevalence of violence leading up to, during, and, particularly, after an election is important when examining press freedom. As was discussed in Chapter 4, Kenya, for example, has experienced notable post-election violence which led to media restrictions, some of which were short-lived and others of which have remained and permeated government policies and ideologies.

Much has been discussed about media ownership, which is an integral component of the inner workings of a media system, particularly the political and tribal implications of ownership structures. Our interviews with journalists revealed that, because of the political-economic architecture of many media houses in the region (that being the serving of political and financial interests first and foremost), press freedom fluctuates based on who owns each media house, as well as how connected that owner and their party or tribe is to political leadership at local and national levels. However, commercial media houses come with their own influences, too, particularly pressure from advertisers. And interwoven with media ownership concerns are a nation's laws, though arguably the ways in which those laws are interpreted and enforced—which can vary significantly—has as much of an impact, according to journalists in this study, as the laws themselves.

Lastly, international linkages and the vibrancy of a country's civil society are contributing factors to the progression or regression of a country's press freedom environment, which can contribute to and be a result of the local political structures. International connections play an important role in shaping local mediascapes by pushing forward certain agendas and holding politicians accountable, but these linkages (and the resulting ideologies) can sway based on global geopolitical shifts. What Kenyans are seeing is a shift from Western, largely American, influence to a growing Chinese presence. Of course, the degree to which these international linkages and their political and media ideologies seep into a society can depend on the strength (or lack) of a dynamic civil society. The reach of NGOs, the social norms of societies, and journalism cultures (how much a journalist is compensated and whether that is enough to discourage unethical behavior, whether professional journalism organizations have any collective power, etc.) are all factors that can influence development and democratization, and in turn improve and lessen levels of press freedom. Figure 6.1 below shows our proposed factors to consider when examining global media systems.

How the Factors May Enhance Existing Models

The assumption of linear movement toward democratization has drawn criticism to Voltmer's (2013) four-arena framework (Run, 2014) and can similarly apply to other models and classification mechanisms. It has been argued that semi-authoritarian states are not emerging or transitioning democracies, they aren't moving in the direction of democratic consolidation; instead, they are "semi-authoritarian by design, not by default," and they are successful because they allow a certain degree of political and media freedom to give the impression of democratic values but use hidden forms of control to ensure that this veil of freedom does not lead to any real change (Ottaway, 2004, p. 9). In the context of media, a nation can have a vibrant press on the surface—independent media houses and multiple broadcasters, some of which even criticize the government—but "informal measures are put in place to guarantee that such freedom of expression will not destabilise those in power" (Frère, 2015, p. 105). Uganda is a prime example of this.

Frère (2015) suggests that these types of countries and media systems, common in Francophone Africa, should be called "pluralist authoritarian" because they are not moving toward democracy—their political and media systems intentionally combine democratic and authoritarian traits. The classification of "pluralist authoritarian" may seem like

a contradiction at first glance, until a distinction is made between the facade and what lies beneath. In the facade we see a pluralist media landscape, a market open to private initiatives, an absence of a priori control over media content, a diversity of political parties able to interact with media outlets, and journalists who have gained autonomy through the establishment

FACTORS TO CONSIDER WHEN EXAMINING GLOBAL MEDIA SYSTEMS

(A STARTING POINT FOR ENHANCED CONTEXTUALIZATION)

Distance from conflict

How long has it been since the country/community experienced civil conflict?

What scope and depth of conflict did the country/community experience?

Political benchmarks

How long has the president been in power?

Does the country hold regular, free and fair elections? What takes place in the country after elections?

Who owns the majority of media houses in the country and with what editorial impact?

How consistent is the judicial system in its interpretation of laws?

International linkages

How connected is the country to the international community and to what countries/regions?

Growth of vibrant civil society

How many NGOs operate in the country and with what reach?

What are the social norms and personality traits of citizens?

How well paid, trained and resourced are journalists?

How strong are professional journalism organizations in the country?

Figure 6.1 Factors to consider when examining global media systems

of their own principles of conduct, professional organisations and self-regulatory bodies. But behind the façade, media outlets have to face maneuvering from those in power who wish to control the flow of information through direct political pressure, indirect economic obstacles, dominance on the public media, and manipulation of the legal framework and judicial system. (p. 110)

In many ways the term "pluralist authoritarian" accounts for numerous complexities at play in media systems in non-democratic nations. However, by intentionally thinking about specific nations as not moving toward democracy, do we assume a static position?

As our research and that of countless others has shown, events and structures can make a political system stay in place, move toward democratization, or backslide; sometimes these shifting forces can occur simultaneously, and "the dynamics between freedom and control are constantly evolving" (Fielder & Frère, 2018, p. 139). Thus, understanding the lack of linearity in political development allows us to think about how these frameworks can be utilized in more applicable ways. With added nuance, Voltmer's (2013) four arenas—political, economic, social, and professional—may be useful in examining a range of media systems, especially with added specificity regarding how each arena can be operationalized. The factors that emerged from our research, discussed in Chapter 5, could be used as barometers for each of Voltmer's (2013) areas:

- Political: Distance from conflict (and the breadth and duration of that conflict), length and scope of executive power, elections and their aftermath, interpretation and enforcement of laws
- Economic: Media house ownership (and the political and tribal influences that interplay with that ownership)
- Social: International linkages, the presence (or absence) and reach of NGOs in the country, social norms and personality traits of citizens
- Professional: Pay and training of journalists, strength of professional journalism organizations

While our proposed factors provide nuance to Voltmer's (2013) arenas, her framework was created with post-authoritarian states in mind. Thus, perhaps utilizing her arenas as a conceptual base but focusing on our factors and others would enable scholars and practitioners to more accurately consider the components of a nation's media landscape at any given point in time and within any political environment—not just developed democracies or even transitional, post-authoritarian states—rather than trying to fit distinct media systems into set categories based on political type.

Turning to Ibelema et al.'s (2000) logistical model—which proposes that forces either push toward freedom or control—Rwanda could be classified as being in a state of controlled expression, due to strong forces of control and weak forces of freedom. Uganda could be classified as being in a state of conflict, with both strong forces of freedom and control. And Kenya could be classified as being in a state of (relative) freedom of expression, with forces of freedom strong and forces of control weak. However, it is easy to see how these countries—at least Uganda and Kenya—have shifted between different categories over the decades. What is particularly poignant about Ibelema et al.'s (2000) thought process is their view that "it may be advantageous to discuss press systems not so much in terms of whether they are free, in the traditional sense, but whether the logistical casualty/cost for maintaining the marketplace of ideas is high or low" (p. 113). We agree it is useful to talk about press freedom in terms of how strong the two opposing forces are, those pushing toward freedom and those pushing against it. As our research shows, these forces fluctuate significantly. The factors we explore in this book—and succinctly put in question form in Figure 6.1—can be used to help determine the strength or weakness of the forces of freedom and control.

Similarly, when Fielder and Frère (2018) utilized the logistical model (Ibelema et al., 2000) to examine the media systems in three post-conflict African states, they concluded that political interference, financial issues, difficult working conditions, technical challenges, and journalists' self-perceptions most influence journalists. These contributors overlap with our proposed factors, suggesting that they are indeed important elements of media systems in an array of non-Western countries. However, Fielder and Frère's (2018) factors are more directly related to the journalist, whereas we offer influencing factors related to journalists as well as at the extra-media level. In other words, some of our factors (e.g., the amount of links a country has with the international community) are largely about the country generally but affect the news media.

Wrapping Up and Looking Ahead

While there are reasons to believe that Rwanda's forward progress may not continue at the rate and in the direction that it has been moving, as described in Chapter 2, there is cause for (cautious) optimism. Some journalists in Rwanda believe that positive changes, even if small or slow, are occurring between the government and the press. For example, a Kigali-based reporter who asked that we withhold the name of their employer noted a slight change in government–press relations.

> Right now the government is a little bit relaxed. . . . I think they see the role of journalism in ensuring that public funds are not misused. So we've had a very, very good period, but of course there's a little bit [of] censorship when it comes to still covering very sensitive stories. (Journalist 7, personal communication, June 5, 2016)

A reporter in a management role at the commercial outlet Umuseke in Rwanda attributes the slight improvements in press freedom to changing opinions. "I think it's because there are [sic] some development, change of mindsets in the government people. So they are turning, they are seeing that the media is not here to harm or to negatively report what they have done" (Journalist 10, personal communication, May 30, 2016).

However, that optimism wasn't seen from all journalists that we spoke with in Rwanda. The journalist in the management role at Great Lakes Voice said they would like to see the economic and other progress in the country extend to free speech:

> I wish this positive side of the government is supported by giving more freedom, relaxing a bit when it comes to free speech. . . . But if you suppress free speech and you criminalize speech, if you suppress the press— independent press mostly—and when you control political space and you control civil space, to me you are guilty. (Journalist 23, personal communication, June 5, 2016)

That pessimism, or lack of positive change, described by the Great Lakes Voice journalist in Rwanda more closely mirrored discussions with Ugandan journalists about their situation. President Museveni being in office for even longer than President Kagame has not necessarily led to similar positive changes in opinions there, according to journalists. As discussed in Chapter 3, in Uganda, some officials view journalists as a threat and thus restrict their freedom. While changing mindsets like those in Rwanda would be useful, likely what is more important is a change in leadership. When asked what needs to change in order for additional media freedom to come in Uganda, a reporter from Uganda Radio Network merely said, "The government" with a laugh. They elaborated:

> A lot needs to change, really, but all comes from government. We're trying our best to be more professional, because if you look at the caliber of the journalists then and the caliber of the journalists now, there's a lot more training now on the side of the journalist. There's a lot more effort to seek for information, but then, government is also now tightening the rope. (Journalist 17, personal communication, June 7, 2018)

The journalist in a management role at the no-longer-publishing Rwandan outlet, Great Lakes Voice, did, however, express hope for the journalism industry if/when Rwanda is to see political change:

> I hope that when dictatorship is done, journalism will rise again. You cannot kill the press. Nobody has ever succeeded in holding onto the press forever—no country! . . . you can limit it for some certain time when you are in power . . . but not forever. (Journalist 23, personal communication, June 5, 2016)

And an editor at *The Standard* in Kenya, among other interviewees, also believes that Rwanda and Uganda will see changes:

> Every nation has its own turning point, yeah, let me give you an example. . . . Rwanda came from a horrific genocide where they believe that [Paul Kagame] is our savior, our current president. But I'm sure now the dissent has started to—it's beginning to—in small measure, but there are guys who are like, "Oh yeah, you [Kagame] did your part but I think it can't be forever." But I'm sure awhile back it was even unthinkable [that] you can rise up. . . . Maybe at the moment [you cannot rise up] but the fact that they can dare do that shows that they're now also in the phase of getting over— not really forgetting the genocide but like you can have it on our—the kind of—it's called—you know the politicians perfect the fear mongering: "If I leave it will disintegrate." You can only have the masses live in that fear for so long . . . look at Zimbabwe, who thought Robert Mugabe would go home? . . . Look at Uganda, the dissent is now picking up. . . . I think every nation has its own phase, maybe now the level at which they are

in is where we were. Because one thing I can tell you for sure, for all the problems we have in Kenya you cannot turn back the clock to that authoritarian system. . . . So [Rwanda and Uganda] will get there but it takes time. (Journalist 6, personal communication, February 27, 2019)

Voltmer (2012) suggests that perhaps some young democracies are not moving in the direction of the liberal model of the Western world and will, instead, function in a hybrid-democratic form that we do not yet understand, and along with that will come different forms of hybrid journalism. Perhaps one or more of the countries examined in this book are currently operating in one of these hybrid journalism ecosystems, or will be in the future.

In Hallin and Mancini's *Comparing Media Systems: Beyond the Western World*, Hadland (2012) suggests that "Africa has a contribution to make to the Hallin–Mancini hypothesis and that fertile ground exists for the design of an alternative model or models populated by the experiences and dynamics of postcolonial African democracies" (pp. 111–112). The previously mentioned factors have been shown to influence media systems in East Africa. While other characteristics surely impact these and other media systems, thus reinforcing the importance of considering each country's individual context when evaluating press freedom and media systems more broadly, these factors, coupled with work by others, specifically Nisbet and Moehler (2005) and Voltmer (2013), can serve as a foundation or basis from which an alternative model or models can be built. Ultimately, though, we should be engaging with the factors that influence media systems, and the fluctuating hybridity, rather than focusing on specific press freedom rankings or classifications.

In sum, as discussed in Chapter 1, many normative theories of the press have overlooked mediascapes from outside North America and Europe, and even those that have factored in nations from other regions have a tendency to be underpinned by a flawed presumption that nations develop in a linear fashion—from non-democracy to democracy, and in doing so, from a restricted press to a free press. The complicated nature of political (and media) change—the ups and downs, forward leaps and quick backslides—calls for more historically informed views of media systems and interpretations of press freedom. Further, mass communication research becomes problematic when it overlooks developing nations and can result in inaccurate conceptualizations of how and why media systems function and with what implications. The Western-dominated hegemonic underpinnings and lack of nuance from which much existing work is based leads to faulty understandings of global media and gives the impression that media systems associated with mature democracies and Western ways of thinking are commonplace.

Drawing on qualitative fieldwork and a cross-national survey, we put forward updated states of the media in Rwanda, Uganda, and Kenya and demonstrated how each nation's political and cultural intricacies complicate traditional media systems frameworks and notions of press freedom. Again, much of the existing media and communication scholarship that has attempted to classify media systems around the world has overlooked the world's most developing nations, particularly those in Africa, and those that have focused specifically on developing nations have been constructed, in part, on the assumption of linear democratization. The ebb and flow of political change, democratization, and backsliding often makes such an assumption inapplicable, or at least uncontextualized. It is our hope that the set of considerations we extrapolated from interviews with and surveys of journalists will push forward media systems frameworks and press classification approaches by more accurately accounting for diverse political environments outside of the Western world. And we hope scholars, practitioners, activists, and media consumers will expand upon our list of factors to make them—and related conversations—more nuanced and comprehensive.

APPENDIX

Methods

The fieldwork that laid the groundwork for this book included in-depth interviews with journalists in Rwanda, Uganda, and Kenya as well as a survey of journalists in each of those three countries. In total, we connected with more than 500 journalists. This appendix includes detailed information about the methods of our research.

Interviews

We conducted semi-structured, in-depth interviews with journalists in Rwanda, Uganda, and Kenya from 2016 through 2019. In-depth interviews have been referred to as "one of the most powerful methods" in qualitative research because they give researchers the opportunity to "step into the mind of another person, to see and experience the world as they do themselves" (McCracken, 1988, p. 9). Journalists, in particular, "represent excellent candidates for qualitative interview projects" (Besley & Roberts, 2010, p. 70) because they should be able to clearly convey their beliefs and experiences, given their profession (Lindlof & Taylor, 2002). We continued conducting interviews in each country until we reached saturation, the point where "additional data do not lead to any new emergent themes" (Given, 2016, p. 135). This amounted to at least two dozen interviews in each country. See Table A.1 for the number of interviews, time frame, and location of interviews for each country.

Sampling and Recruitment

Journalists eligible to be interviewed for this research had to be at least 18 years of age and living in Rwanda, Uganda, or Kenya. We considered a journalist to be someone who was employed (full- or part-time) by a for-profit, non-profit, or government-run media organization. Most of the interviewees were working as reporters or editors, although some participants held other or multiple positions and a few were former journalists.

An effort was made to include a diverse set of journalists, including both men and women, young and old, and those who worked for various platforms (radio, TV, newspapers, online media). We also made sure to include participants from both public and privately owned media houses. The bulk of the journalists worked for local or national news outlets, but a few correspondents from international media outlets were included in each country. See Tables A.2, A.3, and A.4 for the interviewees' job titles, employers, and employer types for each country.

Participants in Rwanda were recruited by the researchers blindly contacting them at first, and a snowball sample ensued. Journalists were identified by conducting searches of Rwandan news outlets' websites for journalist contact information. A later search of social media sites was used to contact additional reporters and editors. These initial journalists were then asked to suggest other journalists who might be interested in participating

Table A.1 Interview Details

Country	Number of interviews	When interviews occurred	Where interviews occurred
Rwanda	24	May and June 2016	Kigali and Butare, Rwanda
Uganda	27	June 2018	Kampala and Luwero, Uganda
Kenya	33	February and March 2019	Nairobi and Nakuru, Kenya

in our study. The samples in Uganda and Kenya were constructed with the help of a local journalist or journalism educator who used their professional network to recruit participants. We worked with each of them to ensure that the sample included a variety of journalists in terms of age, gender, news beat, platform, and type of outlet (e.g., public, private, religious, student). The journalists who participated did not receive any incentive, financial or otherwise. Journalists' names are withheld to protect them from potential retribution, and, at the request of specific individuals, employer names may also be withheld.

Interview Process

All interviews were conducted in English, and all but one (which was done by phone) were conducted in person in either the capital city or a smaller city within a few hours' drive from the capital in each country. The interviews occurred at a location chosen by the participant. Most took place at the office of the interviewee or at a nearby coffee shop. Each interview began with a summary of the study and an informed consent protocol, and they averaged about 45 minutes. Each was audio-recorded with permission, and we also took detailed notes.

The interview questions were open-ended. Journalists were asked to reflect on their own stories and on their role in society and to talk about the challenges they faced in navigating political, economic, and professional pressures. We asked them to share their perceptions of press freedom in their country and how the media have influenced the country's development. We also asked some demographic questions.

Analysis

Transcriptions were created from the audio recordings, which generated 879 typed pages of interview data across the three countries. We read each transcript and its accompanying field notes multiple times to identify central themes, references, or terminology in order to make meaning of the diverse perspectives—a process Baxter and Babbie (2003) refer to as the "iterative cycle" of developing codes by "each time revising the coding categories until they capture all" of the relevant data (p. 367). After an initial set of categories emerged which allowed the data to be organized in a logical and useful way, transcriptions of the interviews were imported as text files into Dedoose, qualitative data analysis software

Table A.2 Rwanda: Interviewee, Job Title, Employer, and Type of Organization

Participant	Job Title	Employer	Type of Org.
Journalist 1	Former Radio/TV Presenter	Voice of Africa*	Religious
Journalist 2	Editor	Radio/TV 10	Commercial
Journalist 3	Online News Editor	Izuba Rirashe	Government
Journalist 4	Senior Producer	Radio/TV 10	Commercial
Journalist 5	Former journalist	Withheld	Government
Journalist 6	Editor/Reporter/ Presenter	Radio Isango Star	Commercial
Journalist 7	Reporter	Withheld	Commercial
Journalist 8	Reporter	The New Times	Gov./Commercial
Journalist 9	Editor	Umusingi	Commercial
Journalist 10	Management role	Umuseke.rw	Commercial
Journalist 11	Journalist	Royal FM	Commercial
Journalist 12	Reporter	The New Times	Gov./Commercial
Journalist 13	Editor	Gusenga.org	Religious
Journalist 14	Senior Reporter	Izuba Rirashe	Government
Journalist 15	Reporter	City Radio	Commercial
Journalist 16	Freelancer	The New Times	Gov./Commercial
Journalist 17	News Editor	The East African*	Commercial
Journalist 18	Reporter	Associated Press*	Commercial
Journalist 19	Former journalist	Withheld	Government
Journalist 20	Management role	Radio Salus	Student
Journalist 21	Reporter	Radio Salus	Student
Journalist 22	Reporter	Kigali Today/KT Radio	Commercial
Journalist 23	Management role	Great Lakes Voice	Commercial
Journalist 24	Editor	Kigali Today	Commercial

Note. The "type of organization" variable is meant to help readers better understand the context surrounding each media house. We tried, when possible, to determine the ownership structure of each outlet; namely, independent versus government funded. However, making this determination proved to be difficult in all three countries but especially in Rwanda. For most outlets in Rwanda, we used the employer type determined by Bonde et al. (2015), but we also relied on interview data. Many media houses in Rwanda are technically independent, yet they rely on the government for the majority of their advertising revenue, blurring the lines between public and private. Further, *The New Times* is known among journalists and the public as a state newspaper, yet an editor at the paper said the outlet is privately owned and not government funded (personal communication, June 8, 2021). The editor did not respond when we asked who owned the newspaper and/or who the shareholders are. As mentioned in Chapter 1, in a survey of Rwandan journalists, more than one third of respondents said that ownership of media is not transparent in the country (Bonde et al., 2015). As a result of these complexities, the "type of organization" variable is determined in-part by each news outlet's funding structure, where available, and in-part by its editorial leaning. Further, a designation of "Gov./Commercial" indicates a mixed funding structure. For example, Urban TV in Uganda is owned by Vision Media Group, which is more than 50% owned by government and the remaining percentage by private individuals.

* Foreign news outlet (not headquartered in the country where the interview occurred)

(see Dedoose.com for more information), to further analyze how frequently and in what capacities those themes, ideas, and phrases were used. Roughly a few dozen codes and subcodes were created for each country's data. A combination of the data being analyzed by real people and computer-supported analysis software enabled the interviews to be categorized by themes and terminology used as well as to account for timing/spacing, tone, and body language.

Surveys

In addition to our interviews with journalists, we conducted a survey of journalists in Rwanda, Uganda, and Kenya to reach a wider audience. In advance of launching the full survey, a pilot study was done in each country in which local journalists from each nation completed a draft of the survey and provided feedback. The final survey was conducted in 2019, with the first email sent to participants in May, followed by subsequent emailed requests for completion into June. The survey was conducted in English and administered online.

Sampling and Recruitment

As with the interviews, this survey did not strive for statistically representative samples, but instead aimed to reach journalists in each country who work for a wide variety of platforms (print, television, radio, online) with various ownership structures (public, private, religious, etc.). In the months preceding the pilot test, lists of journalists' names and email addresses in each country were compiled by searching media outlet websites, social media platforms, journalist association lists, and by harnessing our existing networks to ask for contacts.

Journalists were contacted via email and were invited to participate. Those who completed the survey were offered the chance to win one of two distributions of approximately $50 USD (45,000 Francs, 190,000 UG Shillings, or 5,000 KE Shillings, depending on the country and exchange rates at the time). Winners were later selected using a random number generator, and the money was wired to them and they collected it at their nearest Western Union location. The survey was sent to 2,134 journalists (565 in Rwanda, 821 in Uganda, and 748 in Kenya). In the end, our valid sample included 424 journalists (174 in Rwanda, 148 in Uganda, and 102 in Kenya), resulting in a response rate of 19.9% (30.8% in Rwanda, 18% in Uganda, and 13.6% in Kenya).

Participants

The journalists included in the final sample were experienced and educated. They reported an average of 10 years working in the news business, and 81.4% (of the 73% of the sample who answered the question) said they had studied journalism or mass communication after secondary school. They were mostly reporters (46.3%) or editors (24.6%) and covered a range of topics, primarily investigations (35.6%) and breaking news (15.1%). They worked most in radio (29.7%) but were spread across online (17.9%), daily newspapers (15.4%), television (14.9%), and other media as well. Three fourths of them

Table A.3 Uganda: Interviewee, Job Title, Employer, and Type of Organization

Participant	Job Title	Employer	Type of Org.
Journalist 1	Editor	Daily Monitor	Commercial
Journalist 2	Former journalist	Human Rights Network for Journalists	NGO
Journalist 3	Reporter	NBS	Commercial
Journalist 4	Reporter	Daily Monitor	Commercial
Journalist 5	Photojournalist	Daily Monitor	Commercial
Journalist 6	Reporter	Daily Monitor	Commercial
Journalist 7	Editor/Reporter	Monitor Publications Ltd.	Commercial
Journalist 8	Management role	CEO Magazine	Commercial
Journalist 9	Journalist	Eagle Online	Commercial
Journalist 10	Senior Reporter	New Vision	Government
Journalist 11	Anchor/Reporter	Urban TV	Gov./Commercial
Journalist 12	Reporter	Name withheld	Government
Journalist 13	Reporter	Agence France-Presse*	Commercial
Journalist 14	Photojournalist	Agence France-Presse*	Commercial
Journalist 15	Reporter	Uganda Radio Network	Commercial
Journalist 16	Journalist	Buganda Broadcasting Service (BBS)	Gov./Commercial
Journalist 17	Reporter	Uganda Radio Network	Commercial
Journalist 18	Former reporter	Uganda Hub for Investigative Media	NGO
Journalist 19	Videographer	BBC*	Gov./Commercial
Journalist 20	Photojournalist	New Vision	Government
Journalist 21	Journalist	Daily Monitor	Commercial
Journalist 22	Journalist	Chimp Reports	Commercial
Journalist 23	Correspondent	Daily Monitor	Commercial
Journalist 24	Reporter	Uganda Radio Network	Commercial
Journalist 25	Reporter	Bukedde TV	Government
Journalist 26	Journalist	NTV	Commercial
Journalist 27	Management role	The East African*	Commercial

* Foreign news outlet (not headquartered in the country where the interview occurred)

(74.5%) worked for national news outlets; the rest worked for community media, international outlets, multiple types, or something else. About two-thirds (65.7%) worked for commercial media houses, 18% worked for public media houses, and the rest had a different ownership structure, such as being a religious outlet, student media house, or an

Table A.4 Kenya: Interviewee, Job Title, Employer, and Type of Organization

Participant	Job Title	Employer	Type of Org.
Journalist 1	Editor	MT Kenya Star	Commercial
Journalist 2	News anchor/sub-editor	Hot 96 FM	Commercial
Journalist 3	Reporter	The Standard	Commercial
Journalist 4	Sub-editor	Taifa Leo	Commercial
Journalist 5	Editor/reporter	Citizen Radio	Commercial
Journalist 6	Editor	The Standard	Commercial
Journalist 7	Reporter	Taifa Leo	Commercial
Journalist 8	Reporter/News Anchor	NTV	Commercial
Journalist 9	Reporter	Business Daily	Commercial
Journalist 10	Deputy News Editor	People Daily	Commercial
Journalist 11	Magazine/Features Editor	People Daily	Commercial
Journalist 12	Sub-editor	People Daily	Commercial
Journalist 13	Revise Editor	People Daily	Commercial
Journalist 14	Reporter	Daily Nation	Commercial
Journalist 15	Reporter	KTN News	Commercial
Journalist 16	Reporter	The Standard	Commercial
Journalist 17	Reporter	The Nairobian	Commercial
Journalist 18	Editor	NTV	Commercial
Journalist 19	Reporter	Daily Nation	Commercial
Journalist 20	Managing Editor	Citizen Radio	Commercial
Journalist 21	Reporter	China Daily*	Government
Journalist 22	Bureau Chief	People Daily	Commercial
Journalist 23	Reporter	Radio Amani	Religious
Journalist 24	Presenter	Taach FM Radio	Commercial
Journalist 25	Presenter	Radio Waumini	Religious
Journalist 26	Chief News Editor	KBC	Government
Journalist 27	Associate Editor	Nairobi Business Monthly	Commercial
Journalist 28	Reporter	Kibera News Network	Community
Journalist 29	Digital Reporter	CNN*	Commercial
Journalist 30	Editor-in-chief	KBC	Government
Journalist 31	Reporter	Voice of America*	Government
Journalist 32	Reporter/News Anchor	BBC*	Gov./ Commercial
Journalist 33	Reporter	Habari Kibra	Community

* Foreign news outlet (not headquartered in the country where the interview occurred)

NGO/donor-funded organization. Nearly half (46%) of respondents said the circulation size of their media houses was more than 500,000.

Overall, at least among the participants who answered the demographic questions, the samples leaned toward young to middle-aged, educated males. See Table A.5 for country-level data on gender and age as well as income, experience, and education as it relates to journalism.

Measures

The questionnaire was developed using Qualtrics, an American survey software company. It began with an informed consent protocol, including a confirmation that respondents were 18 years of age or older, after which respondents were asked a series of questions related to their work in the journalism industry, such as their primary role in the newsroom, topics they primarily cover, how long they have worked in the industry, and what type of platform they work for, and information about the size and ownership of the organization they are affiliated with.

The questionnaire then asked participants a series of questions about how they view journalism's role in society, professionalism and challenges in the industry, how news media relate to the development of the country, and questions about public trust in media and their perceptions about past, current, and future levels of press freedom in their country. The survey ended with demographic questions. The IBM SPSS Statistics software was used to analyze the survey data to examine within- and between-country similarities and differences.

Ethics Approvals

This research was reviewed and approved by the Institutional Review Boards at the authors' U.S. universities (Virginia Commonwealth University and Regis University) as well as by IRB or other ethical review boards in each country. In Rwanda, the research was approved by the research ethics review committee at the University of Rwanda and the Rwanda National Council for Science and Technology. In Uganda, the research was approved by the School of Social Sciences Research and Ethics Committee (within the College of Humanities and Social Sciences) at Makerere University as well as the Uganda National Council for Science and Technology. In Kenya, the research was approved by the Institutional Review Board at the United States International University–Africa.

Table A.5 Survey Participant Demographics

Country	Gender (% male)	Age (M)	Monthly journalism income	Years in news business (M)
Rwanda (n =174)	86	32.49 (SD =7.02)	175,000 RWF (171 USD)	7.71
Uganda (n =148)	72.9	35.97 (SD =7.98)	1.92 million UGX (511 USD)	9.65
Kenya (n =102)	72.7	39.58 (SD =7.72)	148,000 KES (1,256 USD)	13.59

Bibliography

Abramowitz, M. J. (2017). Freedom of the Press 2017: Press freedom's dark horizon. Freedom House. Retrieved June 16, 2020, from https://freedomhouse.org/report/free dom-press/2017/press-freedoms-dark-horizon

Abuoga, J. B., & Mutere, A. (1988). *The history of the press in Kenya.* African Council on Communication Education.

Acayo, C., & Mnjama, N. (2004). The print media and conflict resolution in Northern Uganda. *African Journal on Conflict Resolution, 4*(1), 27–43. https://www.accord.org. za/ajcr-issues/%EF%BF%BCthe-print-media-and-conflict-resolution-in-northern-uganda/

Adejumobi, S. (2000). Elections in Africa: A fading shadow of democracy? *International Political Science Review/Revue Internationale de Science Politique, 21*(1), 59–73.

Adekoya, F. (2020, January 2). Why Rwanda leaves other African nations behind. *The Guardian.* https://guardian.ng/features/why-rwanda-leaves-other-african-nations-behind/

Adjovi, E. V. (2003). Liberté de la presse et "affairisme" médiatique au Bénin [Press freedom and greedy journalism in Benin]. *Politique Africaine, 92,* 157–172.

African Development Bank. (2020). East Africa Regional Overview. Retrieved July 21, 2000, from https://www.afdb.org/en/countries/east-africa/east-africa-overview

African Development Bank. (2022). African Economic Outlook 2022. Retrieved September 3, 2022, from https://www.afdb.org/en/documents/african-economic-outl ook-2022

Akumu, P. (2014, February 22). Yoweri Museveni: A dictator with nothing left to promise Uganda. *The Guardian.* https://www.theguardian.com/commentisfree/2014/feb/23/ yoweri-museveni-uganda-dictator-anti-gay

Alden, C., Large, D., & Soares de Oliveira, R. (2008). *China returns to Africa: A rising power and a continent embrace.* Hurst.

Allen, K., & Gagliardone, I. (2011). The media map project Kenya: Case study snapshot of donor support to ICTs and media. http://www.mediamapresource.org/wp-content/ uploads/2011/04/Kenya_web1.pdf

Altschull, J. H. (1984). *Agents of power: The role of the news media in human affairs.* Longman.

Amah, M. (2018, April 26). US-owned Christian radio station in Rwanda shut down for saying women are evil. CNN. https://www.cnn.com/2018/04/26/africa/radio-station-shutdown-rwanda-africa/index.html

Ambala, A. T. (2014). Reimagining the Kenyan television broadcasting-scape: Active user-generated content (AUGC) as an emancipating platform. *Ecquid Novi: African Journalism Studies, 35*(3), 39–53.

Ambala, A. T. (2016). Voicing "Kenyanness" in the everyday: Disrupting traditional broadcasting tropes through participatory digital storytelling. *African Journalism Studies, 37*(4), 45–61.

Amnesty International. (2010, August 31). Rwanda: Vague laws used to criminalise criticism of government. https://www.amnesty.org/en/latest/press-release/2010/08/18403/

Anite, C., & Nkuubi, J. (2014). Media freedom in Uganda: Analysis of inequitable legal limitations. Human Rights Network for Journalists–Uganda.

Arieff, A. (2019). Rwanda: In brief. Congressional Research Service. Retrieved June 1, 2020, fromhttps://fas.org/sgp/crs/row/R44402.pdf

Arseneault, M. (2013, September 9). Kenyan radio host faces ICC trial on hate speech charges. Radio France Internationale. https://www.rfi.fr/en/africa/20130909-kenyan-radio-journalist-trial-icc

Article 19. (2018, May 2). Kenya: Violations of media freedom 2017–18. Article 19. https://www.article19.org/resources/kenya-violations-media-freedom/

Balaton-Chrimes, S. (2021). Who are Kenya's 42(+) tribes? The census and the political utility of magical uncertainty. *Journal of Eastern African Studies, 15*(1), 43–62.

Banda, F. (2007). An appraisal of the applicability of development journalism in the context of public service broadcasting (PSB). *Communicatio, 33*(2), 154–170.

Baxter, L. A., & Babbie, E. R. (2003). The basics of communication research. Wadsworth/Cengage Learning.

BBC. (2010, June 25). Rwanda "assassins" kill reporter Jean Leonard Rugambage. https://www.bbc.com/news/10413793

BBC. (2022, April 12). Kenya Media Guide. Retrieved March 30, 2023, from https://www.bbc.com/news/world-africa-13681344

BBC Media Action. (2019). Uganda—Media Landscape Report. https://www.communityengagementhub.org/wp-content/uploads/sites/2/2019/09/Uganda-Media-Landscape-report_BBC-Media-Action_February-2019.pdf

BBC Monitoring Database. (2008). Kenya: A brief guide to the media. January. (Cited in Ismail & Deane, 2008)

Becker, L. B., Vlad, T., & Nusser, N. (2007). An evaluation of press freedom indicators. *International Communication Gazette, 69*(1), 5–28.

Beresford, A., Berry, M. E., & Mann, L. (2018). Liberation movements and stalled democratic transitions: Reproducing power in Rwanda and South Africa through productive liminality. *Democratization, 25*(7), 1231–1250.

Berger, G. (2010). Problematizing "media development" as a bandwagon gets rolling. *International Communication Gazette, 72*(7), 547–565.

Berman, A. (2016, April 22). Dictator in disguise. *Harvard Political Review*. https://harvardpolitics.companylogogenerator.com/world/your-friendly-neighborhood-dictator/

Besley, J. C., & Roberts, M. C. (2010). Qualitative interviews with journalists about deliberative public engagement. Journalism Practice, 4(1), 66–81.

Blankenberg, N. (1999). In search of real freedom: Ubuntu and the media. *Critical Arts, 12*(2), 42–65.

Bloomberg. (2014, July 1). People Daily offers free newspaper. *Capital Business*. https://www.capitalfm.co.ke/business/2014/07/people-daily-offers-free-newspaper/

Bloomfield, S. (2008, January 23). Kibaki "stole" Kenyan election through vote-rigging and fraud. *The Independent*. https://www.independent.co.uk/news/world/africa/kibaki-stole-kenyanelection-through-vote-rigging-and-fraud-772349.html

Bonde, B. N., Uwimana, J.-P., Sowa, F., & O'Neil, G. (2015). *The state of media freedom in Rwanda*. Rwanda Media Commission. https://rsf.org/sites/default/files/6_5_2015_ib_-_final_report_on_state_of_the_media_freedom_in_rwanda_00.00.pdf

Bowman, W. M., & Bowman, J. D. (2016). Censorship or self-control? Hate speech, the state and the voter in the Kenyan election of 2013. *Journal of Modern African Studies, 54*(3), 495–531.

Boyd-Barrett, O. (1980). *The international news agencies.* Constable.

Bratton, M., Mattes, R., & Gyimah-Boadi, E. (2005). *Public opinion, democracy, and market reform in Africa.* Cambridge University Press.

Bratton, M., & van de Walle. (1994). Neopatrimonial regimes and political transitions in Africa. *World Politics, 46*(4), 453–489.

Brenan, M. (2021, October 27). Americans' trust in media dips to second lowest on record. Gallup. https://news.gallup.com/poll/355526/americans-trust-media-dips-sec ond-lowest-record.aspx

Breunig, C. (1994). Kommunikationsfreiheiten: Ein internationaler Vergleich [Communication freedoms: An international comparison]. Universitaetsverlag Konstanz.

Bromley, R. (2007). Beast, vermin, insect: "Hate" media and the construction of the enemy—The case of Rwanda, 1990–1994. In N. Billias & L. Praeg (Eds.), *Creating destruction: Constructing images of violence and genocide* (pp. 39–60). Rodopi.

Buchholz, K. (2022, February 9). The countries with the most women in national parliament. Statista. Retrieved July 18, 2022, from https://www.statista.com/chart/16919/ share-of-women-in-the-lower-house-of-parliament/

Buehler, M. (2013). Safety-valve elections and the Arab Spring: The weakening (and resurgence) of Morocco's Islamist Opposition Party. *Terrorism and Political Violence, 25*(1), 137–156. https://doi.org/10.1080/09546553.2013.733274

Bujo, B. (2001). *Foundations of an African ethic: Beyond the universal claims of Western morality* (B. McNeil, Trans.). Crossroad Publishing.

Burnet, J. E. (2012). *Genocide lives in us: Women, memory, and silence in Rwanda.* University of Wisconsin Press.

Business Today. (2018, February 28). Why Uhuru rejected Moi's Sh3.5bn price to sell standard. *Business Today.* https://businesstoday.co.ke/uhurus-failed-quest-standard-group-moi-nation/

Cascais, A. (2020, April 17). 20 years under Rwanda's "benevolent dictator" Paul Kagame. *Deutsche Welle.* https://www.dw.com/en/20-years-under-rwandas-benevolent-dicta tor-paul-kagame/a-53159121

Center for Conflict Management of the National University of Rwanda. (2012). *Evaluation of gacaca process: Achieved results per objective.* National Service of Gacaca Courts.

Central Intelligence Agency. (2019). The world factbook. Explore All Countries: Rwanda. Retrieved March 28, 2020, from https://www.cia.gov/the-world-factbook/countries/ rwanda/

Chasi, C., & Rodny-Gumede, Y. (2021). Rethinking peace journalism in light of *ubuntu.* In J. Maweu & A. Mare (Eds.), *Media, conflict and peacebuilding in Africa* (pp. 19–30). Routledge.

Chaudhury, D. R. (2021, December 11). China's influence on African media: Challenge for continent's democracies. *The Economic Times.* https://economictimes.indiatimes. com/news/international/world-news/chinas-influence-on-african-media-challenge-for-continents-democracies/articleshow/88222523.cms?utm_source=contentofinter est&utm_medium=text&utm_campaign=cppst

Cheeseman, N., Maweu, J., & Ouma, S. (2019). Peace but at what cost? Media coverage of elections and conflict in Kenya. In K. Voltmer, C. Christensen, I. Neverla, N. Stremlau,

B. Thomass, N. Vladisavljevic, & H. Wasserman (Eds.), *Media, communication and the struggle for democratic change* (pp. 83–105). Palgrave Macmillan.

Chhokar, J. S., Brodbeck, F. C., & House, R. J. (Eds.). (2008). *Culture and leadership across the world: The GLOBE book of in-depth studies of 25 societies* (Organization and Management Series). Taylor & Francis Group.

Chibita, M. (2009). The politics of broadcasting, language policy and democracy in Uganda. *Journal of African Media Studies, 1*(2), 295–307.

Chibita, M., & Fourie, P. J. (2007). A socio-history of the media and participation in Uganda. *Communicatio, 33*(1), 1–25. https://doi.org/10.1080/02500160701398938

Chikwanha, A. B. (2007). The anatomy of conflicts in the East African Community (EAC): Linking security with development. https://www.ascleiden.nl/Pdf/LectureAnn ieChikwanha.pdf

Christians, C. (2000). Social dialogue and media ethics. *Ethical Perspectives, 7*(2&3), 182–193.

Christians, C. (2004). Ubuntu and communitarianism in media ethics. *Ecquid Novi, 25*(2), 235–256.

Christians, C., Glasser, T., McQuail, D., Nordenstreng, K., & White, R. (2009). *Normative theories of the media: Journalism in democratic societies.* University of Illinois Press.

Coalition for the International Criminal Court. (n.d.). William Ruto and Joshua Sang. Coalition for the International Criminal Court. https://www.coalitionfortheicc.org/ cases/william-ruto-and-joshua-sang

Collins, K. (2013, November 4). Exclusive: Rwanda's "digital president" Paul Kagame on technology's role in Africa's future. *Wired.* https://www.wired.co.uk/article/paul-kag ame-exclusive-interview

Colton, T., & Skach, C. (2005). The Russian predicament. *Journal of Democracy, 16*(3), 113–126.

Committee to Protect Journalists. (2007, February 5). Attacks on the press 2006: Uganda. Committee to Protect Journalists. https://cpj.org/2007/02/attacks-on-the-press-2006- uganda/

Committee to Protect Journalists. (2015). Broken promises: How Kenya is failing to uphold its commitment to a free press. Committee to Protect Journalists. https:// cpj.org/reports/2015/07/broken-promises-kenya-failing-to-uphold-commitm ent-to-free-press/

Committee to Protect Journalists. (2022). Rwanda. Retrieved November 11, 2022, fromhttps://cpj.org/data/killed/africa/rwanda/

Dallaire, R. (2019). The media and the Rwanda genocide. In A. Thompson (Ed.), *Media and mass atrocity: The Rwanda genocide and beyond* (pp. 17–31). McGill-Queens University Press.

de Beer. (2019). Ubuntu, reconciliation in Rwanda, and returning to personhood through collective narrative. In J. Ogude (Ed.), *Ubuntu and the reconstitution of community* (pp. 185–205). University of Indiana Press.

de Lame, D. (2013). Mighty secrets, public commensality, and the crisis of transparency: Rwanda through the looking glass. *Canadian Journal of African Studies, 38*(2), 279–317.

Des Forges, A. (1999). *Leave none to tell the story.* Human Rights Watch.

Dicklitch, S., & Lwanga, D. (2003). The politics of being non-political: Human rights organizations and the creation of a positive human rights culture in Uganda. *Human Rights Quarterly, 25*(2), 482–509.

Domatob, J. K., & Hall, S. W. (1983). Development journalism in black Africa. *Gazette,* *31*(1), 9–33.

Doochin, D. (2019, August 31). What languages are spoken in Kenya? Babbel. Retrieved May 18, 2020, fromhttps://www.babbel.com/en/magazine/what-language-is-spo ken-in-kenya

Doyle, M. (2019). Reporting the genocide. In A. Thompson (Ed.), *Media and mass atrocity: The Rwanda genocide and beyond* (pp. 33–52). McGill-Queens University Press.

Edwin, D. (2022, January 21). Explore Uganda, The pearl of Africa campaign launched. NBS. https://nbs.ug/2022/01/explore-uganda-the-pearl-of-africa-campaign- launched/

Einashe, I. (2016). Living in fear for reporting on terror: A Kenyan journalist speaks out after going into hiding. *Index on Censorship, 45*(2), 31–33.

Eramian, L. (2017). *Peaceful selves: Personhood, nationhood, and the post-conflict moment in Rwanda.* Berghahn Books.

Ess, C. (2013). *Digital media ethics* (2nd ed.). Polity Press.

Fiedler, A., & Frère, M.-S. (2018). Press freedom in the African Great Lakes region: A comparative study of Rwanda, Burundi, and the Democratic Republic of Congo. In H. Mabweazara (Ed.), *Newsmaking cultures in Africa* (pp. 119–143). Palgrave Macmillan.

Fisher, J., & Anderson, D. M. (2015). Authoritarianism and the securitization of develop- ment in Africa. *International Affairs, 91*(1), 131–151.

Flanagan, J. (2018). Rwanda's president Kagame is a despot in disguise, says critic facing jail. *The Times.* https://www.thetimes.co.uk/article/rwanda-s-president-kagame-is-a- despot-in-disguise-says-critic-facing-jail-ljgz3hst0

Fourie, P. (2011). Normative media theory in a changed media landscape and globalized society. In N. Hyde-Clarke (Ed.), *Communication and media ethics in South Africa* (pp. 25–45). Juta.

Fox, K. (2019, July 27). Opposition members keep going "missing" in Rwanda. Few ex- pect them to return. CNN. https://www.cnn.com/2019/07/27/africa/rwanda-opposit ion-disappearances-intl/index.html

Freedom House. (2017). Freedom in the world 2017: Uganda. Retrieved April 4, 2020, fromhttps://freedomhouse.org/country/uganda/freedom-world/2017

Freedom House. (2022a). Freedom in the world 2022: Rwanda. Retrieved November 2, 2022, from https://freedomhouse.org/country/rwanda/freedom-world/2022

Freedom House. (2022b). Freedom in the world 2022: Uganda. Retrieved November 3, 2022, fromhttps://freedomhouse.org/country/uganda/freedom-world/2022

Frère, M.-S. (2009). After the hate media: Regulation in the DRC, Burundi and Rwanda. *Global Media and Communication, 5*(3), 327–352.

Frère, M.-S. (2015). Francophone Africa: The rise of "pluralist authoritarian" media sys- tems?. *African Journalism Studies, 36*(1), 103–112.

Gandhi, J., & Lust-Okar, E. (2009). Elections under authoritarianism. *Annual Review of Political Science, 12*, 403–422.

Gariyo, Z. (1993). *The media, constitutionalism, and democracy in Uganda.* Centre for Basic Research.

Gicheru, C. (2021, June 23). 2021 Digital news report: Kenya. Reuters Institute for the Study of Journalism. https://reutersinstitute.politics.ox.ac.uk/digital-news-report/2021/kenya

Gimson, S. (2017, May). It's not just Trump: US media freedom fraying at the edges: A review of threats to press freedom. Index on Censorship. https://www.indexoncensors hip.org/not-just-trump-us-media-freedom-fraying-edges/

Githiora, C. (2008). Kenya: Language and the search for a coherent national identity. In A. Simpson (Ed.), *Language and national identity in Africa* (pp. 235–251). Oxford University Press.

Given, L. M. (2016). 100 questions (and answers) about qualitative research. SAGE Publications.

Grant, A. M. (2015). Quiet insecurity and quiet agency in post-genocide Rwanda. *Etnofoor, 27*(2), 15–36.

Grzyb, A. (2019, April 1). Debate continues about the media's role in driving Rwanda's genocide. The Conversation. Retrieved May 3, 2020, fromhttps://theconversation.com/debate-continues-about-the-medias-role-in-driving-rwandas-genocide-114512

Gourevitch, P. (2009, April 27). The life after: Fifteen years after the genocide in Rwanda, the reconciliation defies expectations. *The New Yorker.* https://www.newyorker.com/magazine/2009/05/04/the-life-after

Gyekye, K. (1987). *An essay on African philosophical thought.* Cambridge University Press.

Hachten, W. A. (1965). The press in a one-party state: Kenya since independence. *Journalism Quarterly, 42*(3), 262–266.

Hachten, W. A. (1981). *The world news prism: Changing media, changing ideologies.* Iowa State University Press.

Hachten, W. A. (1992). *The world news prism: Changing media in international communication* (3rd ed.). Iowa State University Press.

Hachten, W. A. (1996). *The world news prism: Changing media of international communication* (4th ed.). Iowa State University Press.

Hachten, W. A., & Scotton, J. F. (2012). *The world news prism: Challenges of digital communication* (8th ed.). Wiley-Blackwell.

Hadland, A. (2010). A perspective from the south: Triggers and signs of change. In B. Dobek-Ostrowska, M. Glowacki, K. Jakubowicz, & M. Sükösd, (Eds.), *Comparative media systems: European and global perspectives* (pp. 77–96). Central European University Press.

Hadland, A. (2012). Africanizing three models of media and politics: The South African experience. In D. C. Hallin & P. Mancini (Eds.), *Comparing media systems beyond the Western world* (pp. 96–118). Cambridge University Press.

Hafner-Burton, E., Hyde, S., & Jablonski, R. (2014). When do governments resort to election violence? *British Journal of Political Science, 44*(1), 149–179.

Hallin, D., & Mancini, P. (2004). *Comparing media systems: Three models of media and politics.* Cambridge University Press.

Hallin, D., & Mancini, P. (2012). *Comparing media systems beyond the Western world.* Cambridge University Press.

Hanitzsch, T. (2011). Populist disseminators, detached watchdogs, critical change agents and opportunist facilitators: Professional milieus, the journalistic field and autonomy in 18 countries. *International Communication Gazette, 37*(6), 477–494.

Hanitzsch, T., Seethaler, J., Skewes, E., Anikina, M., Berganza, R., Cangoz, I., Coman, M., Hamada, B., Hanusch, F., Karadjov, C., Mellado, C., Moreira, S., Mwesige, P., Plaisance, P., Reich, Z., Vardiansyah, D., & Yuen, K. (2012). Worlds of journalism: Journalistic cultures, professional autonomy, and perceived influences across 18 nations. In D. Weaver & L. Willnat (Eds.), *The global journalist in the 21st century* (pp. 473–494). Routledge.

Hanitzsch, T., Hanusch, F., Ramaprasad, J., & De Beer, A. S. (Eds.). (2019). *Worlds of journalism: Journalistic cultures around the globe.* Columbia University Press.

Harbeson, J. W., & Rothchild, D. (2009). *Africa in a world of politics* (4th ed.). Westview Press.

Harwood, A., Herrick, E., & Ugangu, W. (2018). Strengthening Kenyan media: Exploring a path towards journalism in the public interest. Retrieved May 14, 2020, from https://kenyamedia.reboot.org/assets/Reboot_Strengthening%20Kenyan%20Media.pdf

He, B. (2001). The national identity problem and democratization: Rustow's theory of sequence. *Government and Opposition, 36*(1), 97–119.

Hinton, S. (2015). The connection between ubuntu indigenous philosophy and the gacaca traditional judicial process in Rwanda. *US-China Education Review, 5*(1), 392–397.

Höglund, C. M., & Schaffer, J. K. (2021). Defending journalism against state repression: Legal mobilization for media freedom in Uganda. *Journalism Studies, 22*(4), 516–534.

Human Rights Network for Journalists-Uganda. (2014, July 18). HRNJ-U Statement: Computer Misuse Act 2011. Human Rights Network for Journalists-Uganda. https://hrnjuganda.wordpress.com/2014/07/18/hrnj-u-statement-computer-misuse-act-2011/

Human Rights Watch. (2008). Ballots to bullets: Organized political violence and Kenya's crisis of governance. Human Rights Watch. https://www.hrw.org/report/2008/03/16/ballots-bullets/organized-political-violence-and-kenyas-crisis-governance

Human Rights Watch. (2010, May 2). A media minefield: Increased threats to freedom of expression in Uganda. Human Rights Watch. https://www.hrw.org/report/2010/05/02/media-minefield/increased-threats-freedom-expression-uganda#_ftnref156

Human Rights Watch. (2012, March 21). Q&A on Joseph Kony and the Lord's Resistance Army. Human Rights Watch. https://www.hrw.org/news/2012/03/21/qa-joseph-kony-and-lords-resistance-army#

Human Rights Watch. (2018). Rwanda: Events of 2017. Human Rights Watch. https://www.hrw.org/world-report/2018/country-chapters/rwanda

Human Rights Watch. (2020). World report 2020: Rwanda. Human Rights Watch. https://www.hrw.org/world-report/2020/country-chapters/rwanda

Human Rights Watch. (2022). Rwanda: Wave of free speech prosecutions. Human Rights Watch. https://www.hrw.org/news/2022/03/16/rwanda-wave-free-speech-prosecutions

Human Rights Watch. (2023, January 20). Rwanda: Suspicious Death of Investigative Journalist. Human Rights Watch. https://www.hrw.org/news/2023/01/20/rwanda-suspicious-death-investigative-journalist

Ibelema, M., Powell, L., & Self, W. R. (2000). Press freedom as a logistical notion. *Free Speech Yearbook, 38*(1), 98–115.

Ibrahim Index of African Governance. (2020). 2020 IIAG. Mo Ibrahim Foundation. https://mo.ibrahim.foundation/sites/default/files/2020-11/2020-index-report.pdf

IGIHE. (2021, February 25). Media High Council phased out. IGIHE.https://en.igihe.com/news/article/media-high-council-phased-out

The Independent. (2021, May 3). Public trust in radio, television content remains consistent—Report. *The Independent.* https://www.independent.co.ug/public-trust-in-radio-television-content-remains-consistent-report/

Ingelaere, B. (2018). *Inside Rwanda's gacaca courts: Seeking justice after genocide.* University of Wisconsin Press.

International Crisis Group. (2004). Northern Uganda: Understanding and solving the conflict. International Crisis Group. https://www.crisisgroup.org/africa/horn-africa/uganda/northern-uganda-understanding-and-solving-conflict

International Institute for Democracy and Electoral Assistance. (2019). The global state of democracy 2019. International IDEA. https://www.idea.int/sites/default/files/publi cations/the-global-state-of-democracy-2019.pdf

International Labour Organization. (2019). Infrastructure development, the construction sector and employment in Rwanda. Retrieved June 8, 2020, from https://www.ilo.org/wcmsp5/groups/public/---ed_emp/---ifp_skills/documents/publication/wcms_723 290.pdf

Internet World Stats. (2022). Internet world stats: Usage and population statistics, Africa. Retrieved November 2, 2022, from https://www.internetworldstats.com/stats1.htm

Ireri, K. (2012). Newspaper visibility of members of parliament in Kenya. *Journalism and Mass Communication, 2*(7), 717–734.

Ireri, K., Chege, N., Kibarabara, J., & Onyalla, D. B. (2019). Frame analysis: Newspaper coverage of Kenya's oil exploration in the post-2012 discovery era. *African Journalism Studies, 40*(2), 34–50.

Iribagiza, G. (2022, April 6). Media watchdog warns against genocide ideology. *The New Times.* https://www.newtimes.co.rw/news/media-watchdog-warns-against-genocide-ideology

Irwin, D., & Kiereini, N. (2021). Media influence on public policy in Kenya. *Journal of Modern African Studies, 59*(2), 159–173.

Ismail, J. A., & Deane, J. (2008). The 2007 general election in Kenya and its aftermath: The role of local language media. *International Journal of Press/Politics, 13*(3), 319–327. https://doi.org/10.1177/1940161208319510

Isoba, J. C. G. (1980). The rise and fall of Uganda's newspaper industry, 1900–1976. *Journalism & Mass Communication Quarterly, 57*(2), 224–233.

Jalloh, A.-B. (2021, September 15). Rwanda: The mysterious deaths of political opponents. DW. https://www.dw.com/en/rwanda-the-mysterious-deaths-of-political-opponents/a-59182275

Jenkins, H. (2006). *Convergence culture: Where old and new media collide.* New York University Press.

Jjuuko, F. (2015). *The 4th estate: Media freedom and rights in Uganda.* Fountain Publishers.

Kabuju, E. (2012, August 28). Bundibugyo Radio sacks 15 workers over tribal clashes. Uganda Radio Network. https://ugandaradionetwork.com/story/bundibugyo-radio-sacks-15-workersover-tribal-clashes

Kagame, P. (2019a, May 15). Address by president Paul Kagame at 5th Transform Africa Summit. http://paulkagame.com/?p=14462

Kagame, P. [@PaulKagame]. (2019b, Dec. 21). Smartphones should not be a luxury item. Let's challenge ourselves to make Smartphones an everyday tool enabling all Rwandans to fulfill their potential. [Tweet]. https://twitter.com/PaulKagame/status/12084966 43605180417

Kagonye, F. (2022, July 5). Uganda adopts Swahili as an official language. *The Sunday Standard.* https://www.standardmedia.co.ke/world/article/2001449634/uganda-ado pts-swahili-as-an-official-language

Kalyango, Y., & Eckler, P. (2010). Media performance, agenda building, and democratiza-tion in East Africa. *Communication Yearbook, 34*(1), 355–389.

Kamilindi, T. (2007). Journalism in a time of hate media. In A. Thompson (Ed.), *The media and the Rwandan genocide* (pp. 136–144). Pluto Press.

Karemera, S. (2019, May 7). Fred Muvunyi is simply a tool of foreign actors. *The New Times.* https://www.newtimes.co.rw/opinions/fred-muvunyi-simply-tool-foreign-actors

Kasoma, F. P. (1995). The role of the independent media in Africa's change to democracy. *Media, Culture & Society, 17*(4), 537–555.

Kayumba, C., & Kimonyo, J. P. (2006). Media assistance to postgenocide Rwanda. In J. de Zeeuw & K. Kumar (Eds.), *Promoting democracy in postconflict societies* (pp. 211–235). Lynne Rienner.

Kenya News Agency. (n.d.). FAQ. Retrieved June 1, 2020, from https://www.kenyan ews.go.ke/faq/#:~:text=The%20Kenya%20News%20Agency%20was,mission%20en ded%20with%20the%20war

Kellow, C. L., & Steeves, H. L. (1998). The role of radio in the Rwandan genocide. *Journal of Communication, 48*(3), 107–128.

Kibuacha, F. (2022, April 26). Top TV and radio stations in Kenya—Q1 2022. GeoPoll. Retrieved June 2, 2022, from https://www.geopoll.com/blog/top-tv-radio-stati ons-kenya-q1-2022/

Kimumwe, P. (2014). *Media regulation and practice in Uganda: A journalist's handbook.* ClearMark.

Kinzer, S. (2010, March 2). The limits of free speech in Rwanda. *The Guardian.* https:// www.theguardian.com/commentisfree/libertycentral/2010/mar/02/rwanda-free-spe ech-genocide

Kinzer, S. (2011, January 27). Kagame's authoritarian turn risks Rwanda's future. *The Guardian.* https://www.theguardian.com/commentisfree/cifamerica/2011/jan/27/rwa nda-freedom-of-speech

Kunczik, M. (1988). *Concepts of journalism north and south.* Friedrich Ebert-Stiftung.

Lacey, M. (2004, April 9). A decade after massacres, Rwanda outlaws ethnicity. *New York Times.* Retrieved from https://www.nytimes.com/2004/04/09/world/a-decade-after-massacres-rwanda-outlaws-ethnicity.html#:~:text=Twahrwa%2C%20a%20H utu%2C%20is%20halfway,we%20think%2C"%20Mr

Lang, M. (2018, February 2). Rwanda's ambition for tech revolution at odds with government control. *San Francisco Chronicle.* https://www.sfchronicle.com/business/article/ Rwanda-s-ambition-for-tech-revolution-at-odds-12548212.php

Lemke, J. (2020). Pushing a political agenda: Harassment of French and African journalists in Côte d'Ivoire's 2010–2011 National Election Crisis. *International Journal of Communication, 14,* 472–490.

Lindlof, T. R., & Taylor, B. C. (2002). Qualitative communication research methods. SAGE.

Linz, J. & Stepan, A. (1996). *Problems of Democratic Transition and Consolidation. South Europe, South America, and Post-Communist Europe.* Johns Hopkins University Press.

Livingston, S. (2007). Limited vision: How both the American media and government failed Rwanda. In A. Thompson (Ed.), *The media and the Rwanda genocide* (pp. 188–197). Pluto Press.

Lodamo, B., & Skjerdal, T. S. (2009). Freebies and brown envelopes in Ethiopian journalism, *Ecquid Novi: African Journalism Studies, 30*(2), 134–154.

Lugalambi, G. W., & Tabaire, B. (2010). Overview of the state of media freedom in Uganda: A research report. *African Centre for Media Excellence.* http://acme-ug.org/ wp-content/uploads/Research-Report-on-State-of-Media-Freedom-in-Uganda.pdf

MacKinnon, R. (2008). Flatter world and thicker walls? Blogs, censorship and civic discourse in China. *Public Choice, 134*(1/2), 31–46.

Madrid-Morales, D. (2021). Who set the narrative? Assessing the influence of Chinese global media on news coverage of COVID-19 in 30 African countries. *Global Media and China, 6*(2), 129–151.

Mäkinen, M., & Wangu Kuira, M. (2008). Social media and postelection crisis in Kenya. *International Journal of Press/Politics, 13*(3), 328–335.

Makokha, K. (2010). The dynamics and politics of media in Kenya: The role and impact of mainstream media in the 2007 general election. In K. Kanyinga & D. Okello (Eds.), *Tensions and reversals in democratic transitions: The Kenya 2007 general elections* (pp. 271–308). University of Nairobi.

Mamdani, M. (1996). *Citizen and subject: Contemporary Africa and the legacy of late colonialism.* Princeton University Press.

Mamdani, M. (2001). *When victims become killers: Colonialism, nativism, and the genocide in Rwanda.* Princeton University Press.

Maractho, E. C. (2015). Broadcasting governance and development in "Museveni's Uganda." *African Journalism Studies, 36*(2), 5–24.

Martin, L. J., & Chaudhary, A. G. (1983). *Comparative mass media systems.* Longman Press.

Masolo, D. A. (2004). Western and African communitarianism: A comparison. In K. Wiredu (Ed.), *Companion to African philosophy* (pp. 483–498). Blackwell.

Matfess, H. (2015). Rwanda and Ethiopia: Developmental authoritarianism and the new politics of African strong men. *African Studies Review, 58*(2), 181–204.

Matovu, J. M., & Stewart, F. (2000). Uganda: The social and economic costs of conflict. In F. Stewart and V. Fitzgerald (Eds.), *War and underdevelopment* (Vol. 2, pp. 240–288). Oxford University Press.

Matupire, P. M. (2017). *Integral ubuntu leadership.* Routledge.

Mbeke, O., Ugangu, W., & Okello-Orlale, R. (2010). *The media we want: Kenya media vulnerabilities study.* Friedrich Ebert Stiftung.

Mbeke, P. (2010). *Mass media in Kenya: Systems and practice.* The Jomo Kenyatta Foundation.

Mboti, N. (2015). May the real ubuntu please stand up? *Journal of Media Ethics, 30*(2), 125–147.

McCombs, M., & Shaw, D. L. (1972). The agenda-setting function of mass media. *Public Opinion Quarterly, 36*(2), 176–187.

McCracken, G. (1988). *The long interview.* SAGE.

McDoom, O. S. (2020). Contested counting: Toward a rigorous estimate of the death toll in the Rwandan genocide. *Journal of Genocide Research, 22*(1), 83–93.

McIntyre, K., & Sobel Cohen, M. (2019, September 10–11). *Journalism practice in Uganda: In a nation transitioning to democracy, challenges remain.* Paper presented at Future of Journalism conference, Cardiff, UK.

McIntyre, K., & Sobel Cohen, M. (2021a). Public trust in state-run news media in Rwanda. *Journalism & Mass Communication Quarterly, 98*(3), 808–827.

McIntyre, K., & Sobel Cohen, M. (2021b). Salary, suppression, and spies: Journalistic challenges in Uganda. *Journalism Studies, 22*(2), 243–261.

McIntyre, K. & Sobel Cohen, M. (2022). Journalistic role orientations in Rwanda, Uganda and Kenya. *International Communication Gazette.* https://doi.org/10.1177/174804 85221141608

McQuail, D. (1983). *Mass communication theory: An introduction.* SAGE.

McQuail, D. (2010). *McQuail's mass communication theory* (6th ed.). SAGE.

McVeigh, T. (2015, December 19). Rwanda votes to give President Paul Kagame right to rule until 2034. *The Guardian.* https://www.theguardian.com/world/2015/dec/20/rwanda-vote-gives-president-paul-kagame-extended-powers

Media Council of Kenya. (2020, November). Status of the media survey. Retrieved March 22, 2021, fromhttps://mediacouncil.or.ke/sites/default/files/downloads/2021-STA TUS%20OF%20THE%20MEDIA%20REPORT.pdf

Meierhenrich, J. (2020). How many victims were there in the Rwandan genocide? A statistical debate. *Journal of Genocide Research, 22*(1), 72–82.

Metz, T. (2011). Ubuntu as a moral theory and human rights in South Africa. *African Human Rights Law Journal, 11*(1), 532–559.

Metz, T. (2015). African ethics and journalism ethics: News and opinion in light of Ubuntu. *Journal of Media Ethics, 30*(2), 74–90.

Metz, T., & Gaie, J. (2010). The African ethic of ubuntu/botho: Implications for research on morality. *Journal of Moral Education, 39*(1), 273–290.

Ministry of Finance (Rwanda). (2017). 7 years government programme: National strategy for transformation. Retrieved June 4, 2020, from https://www.nirda.gov.rw/uploads/ tx_dce/National_Strategy_For_Trsansformation_-NST1-min.pdf

Moemeka, A. A. (1991). *Perspectives on development communication* (African Council for Communication Education). Space Sellers.

Moemeka, A. A. (1994, April). *Socio-cultural dimensions of leadership in Africa.* Paper presented at the Global Majority Retreat, Rocky Hills, CT.

Moemeka, A. A. (1997). Communalistic societies: Community and self-respect as African values. In C. Christians & M. Traber (Eds.), *Communication ethics and universal values* (pp. 170–193). SAGE.

Mokgoro, Y. (1998). Ubuntu and the law in South Africa. *Potchefstroom Electronic Law Journal, 1*, 1–11.

Monks, K. (2019, October 8). Rwanda opens "first entirely homemade" smartphone factory in Africa. CNN. https://www.cnn.com/2019/10/08/africa/rwanda-smartphone-factory/index.html

Moon, R. (2021). When journalists see themselves as villains: The power of negative discourse. *Journalism & Mass Communication Quarterly, 98*(3), 790–807.

Mudge, L. (2021, May 3). What press freedom looks like in Rwanda. Human Rights Watch. Retrieved October 22, 2021, fromhttps://www.hrw.org/news/2021/05/03/what-press-freedom-looks-rwanda#

Muhumuza, R. (2020, April 9). 25 years after genocide, Rwanda's Kagame is praised, feared. Associated Press. https://apnews.com/a97d40a146284383a717aa2ec42eb39b

Muindi, B. (2021). Assessing the impact of terrorism and counter-terrorism laws on freedom of the media in Kenya. In J. Maweu & A. Mare (Eds.), *Media, conflict and peacebuilding in Africa: Conceptual and empirical considerations* (pp. 101–112). Routledge.

Muindi, M. (2020, December 16). Mitigating the impact of media reporting of terrorism—Case study of government communication during Westgate and DusitD2 attacks. International Centre for Counter-Terrorism. Retrieved from https://www.icct. nl/publication/mitigating-impact-media-reporting-terrorism-case-study-governm ent-communication-during

Mukhongo, L. L. (2010). Can the media in Africa shape Africa's political future? *Journal of African Media Studies, 2*(3), 339–352.

Mulligan, G. (2015, April 30). Kenya "gateway to Africa" for US investors—Kenyatta. Disrupt Africa. https://disrupt-africa.com/2015/04/kenya-gateway-to-africa-for-us-investors-kenyatta/

Musa, B. (1997). Uses and abuses of development media theory in sub-Saharan Africa: Critique of a quasi-descriptive/prescriptive theory. *Ecquid Novi*, *18*(1), 132–147.

Musau, D. (2022). William Ruto on press freedom: I welcome criticism from the media. Citizen Digital. https://www.citizen.digital/news/william-ruto-on-press-freedom-i-welcome-criticism-from-the-media-n303980?fbclid=IwAR06mFabTOYXqVkZTJ1YMZn83pwmIQCqK71aDD0YtKrzy4PuHeSNf-mcokU

Musungu, S. F. (2008, January 24). Kenya: Media's role in the election fallout. IPS News. https://www.ipsnews.net/2008/01/kenya-mediarsquos-role-in-the-election-fallout/

Muvunyi, F. (2017, August 1). Don't be fooled by those happy campaign rallies. Rwandans live in fear. *The Washington Post*. https://www.washingtonpost.com/news/democracy-post/wp/2017/08/01/dont-be-fooled-by-those-happy-campaign-rallies-rwandans-live-in-fear/

Mwakideu, C. (2021, January 29). Experts warn of China's growing media influence in Africa. *Deutsche Welle*. https://www.dw.com/en/experts-warn-of-chinas-growing-media-influence-in-africa/a-56385420

Mwakikagile, G. (2007). *Kenya: Identity of a nation*. New Africa.

Mwesige, P. G. (2004). Disseminators, advocates and watchdogs: A profile of Ugandan journalists in the new millennium. *Journalism*, *5*(1), 69–96.

Mwesigwa, D. (2021, July 1). Uganda abandons social media tax but slaps new levy on internet data. The Collaboration on International ICT Policy in East and Southern Africa. https://cipesa.org/2021/07/uganda-abandons-social-media-tax-but-slaps-new-levy-on-internet-data/#:~:text=Introduced%20on%20July%201%2C%202018,Facebook%2C%20Twitter%2C%20and%20WhatsApp.&text=In%20the%20second%20year%2C%20the,a%20paltry%20USD%2016.3%20million.

Mwita, C. (2021). The Kenya media assessment 2021. Internews. https://internews.org/wp-content/uploads/legacy/2021-03/KMAReport_Final_20210325.pdf

Namusoke, E. (2018). Uganda: Press freedom attacked by state bodies. *The Round Table*, *107*(2), 221–223. https://doi.org/ 10.1080/00358533.2018.1448349

Nardone, J. (2010, April 8). Intolerably inferior identity: How the social construction of race erased a Rwandan population. *Peace & Conflict Monitor*. http://www.monitor.upeace.org/archive.cfm?id_article=707

Nassanga, G. (2009). Participatory discussion programs as "hybrid community media" in Uganda. *International Journal of Media & Cultural Politics*, *5*(1/2), 119–124.

Nassanga, G. L., & Tayeebwa, W. (2018). *Assessment of media development in Uganda based on UNESCO media development indicators*. UNESCO.

National Unity and Reconciliation Commission. (2020). NURC background. https://nurc.gov.rw/index.php?id=83

Ndangam, L. (2009). "All of us have taken gombo": Media pluralism and patronage in Cameroonian journalism. *Journalism*, *10*(6), 819–842.

Ndhlovu, L. (2022, April 11). "Brown envelope" journalism in Africa and how to combat it. International Journalists' Network. https://ijnet.org/en/story/brown-envelope-journalism-africa-and-how-combat-it

Nerone, J. (2018, August 28). Four theories of the press. *Oxford Research Encyclopedias: Communication*. Retrieved June 3, 2020, from https://oxfordre.com/communication/view/10.1093/acrefore/9780190228613.001.0001/acrefore-9780190228613-e-815

Nisbet, E., & Moehler, D. (2005, September 1–4). *Emerging political communication systems in Sub-Saharan Africa: Some preliminary models*. Paper presented at the annual meeting of the American Political Science Association, Washington, DC.

Noorlander, P. (2010, August 9). How Paul Kagame has used the law to muzzle Rwanda's media. *The Guardian.* https://www.theguardian.com/law/2010/aug/09/rwanda-paul-kagame-media-censorship

Nsengumukiza, P. (2022, May 6). "Living in constant fear": My 10 years of experience as a journalist in Rwanda. *Jambo News.* https://www.jambonews.net/en/actualites/20220 506-living-in-constant-fear-my-10-years-of-experience-as-a-journalist-in-rwanda/

Nyamnjoh, F. B. (2005). *Africa's media: Democracy and the politics of belonging.* ZED Books.

Nyanjom, O. (2012). *Factually true, legally untrue: Political media ownership in Kenya.* Internews.

Nyeko, O. (2018, July 2). Uganda's troubling social media tax. Human Rights Watch.https://www.hrw.org/news/2018/07/02/ugandas-troubling-social-media-tax

Nyirimanzi, C. (2014, June 5). Rwanda's literacy rate rises. National Institute of Statistics of Rwanda. Retrieved March 21, 2023, from https://www.statistics.gov.rw/publication/rwanda%E2%80%99s-literacy-rate-rises

Obonyo, L. (2003). Kenya. In E. Quick (Ed.), *World press encyclopedia: A survey of press systems worldwide* (pp. 529–539). Gale Group.

Obonyo, L. (2021). Kenya: An exploration of media regulation and accountability. In S. Fengler, T. Eberwein, & M. Karmasin (Eds.), *The global handbook of media accountability* (pp. 313–323). Routledge.

Ochs, M. (1986). *The African press.* The American University in Cairo Press.

Odhiambo, S. (2017). Internet shutdowns during elections. Africa Up Close. https://africa upclose.wilsoncenter.org/internet-shutdowns-during-elections/

Odongo, B. D. (2014). *A critical analysis of the mass media freedom in Uganda.* LAP LAMBERT Academic Publishing.

Ogola, G. (2011a). "If you rattle a snake, be prepared to be bitten": Popular culture, politics and the Kenyan news media. In H. Wasserman (Ed.), *Popular media, democracy and development in Africa* (pp. 123–136). Routledge.

Ogola, G. (2011b). The political economy of the media in Kenya: From Kenyatta's nation-building press to Kibaki's local-language FM radio. *Africa Today, 57*(3), 77–95.

Okeleke, K., & Pedros, X. (2018, July). The mobile economy sub-Saharan Africa 2018. GSMA Intelligence. https://data.gsmaintelligence.com/research/research/research-2018/the-mobile-economy-sub-saharan-africa-2018

Okumbe, M. A., Peel, P. C., Adagala, N., Kowuor, P., & Obonyo, P. L. (2017). An assessment of the Kenyan journalism training and gaps filled by other professionals: A study of selected FM radio stations. *CARI Journals: International Journal of Communication, 1*(2), 1–21. https://doi.org/10.47941/jcomm.126

Oloka-Onyango, J. (2004). "New-breed" leadership, conflict, and reconstruction in the Great Lakes region of Africa. *Africa Today, 50*(3), 29–52.

Onadipe, A., & Lord, D. (1999). Conciliation resources: African media and conflict. New York: Conciliation resources. http://www.c-r.org/occ_papers/af_media/

Oriare, P. M., & Mshindi, T. (2008). Kenya media sector analysis report. Prepared for the Canadian International Development Agency, Nairobi.

Ottaway, M. (2004). *Democracy challenged: The rise of semi-authoritarian state.* Carnegie Endowment for International Peace.

Paris, R. (2004). *At war's end: Building peace after civil conflict.* Cambridge University Press.

Paterson, C. (2011). *The international television news agencies: The world from London.* Peter Lang.

Pinkney, R. (2001). *The international politics of East Africa*. Manchester University Press.

Rakner, L. (2018). Breaking BAD: Understanding backlash against democracy in Africa. Chr. Michelsen Institute. https://www.cmi.no/publications/6518-breaking-bad-understanding-backlash-against

Rao, S., & Wasserman, H. (2007). Global media ethics revisited: A postcolonial critique. *Global Media & Communication, 3*(1), 29–50.

Rayarikar, C. (2017). Rwanda: Development towards authoritarianism? Unpublished thesis, Trinity College. Retrieved May 28, 2020, fromhttps://digitalrepository.trincoll.edu/cgi/viewcontent.cgi?article=1656&context=theses

Reporters Without Borders. (2008, July 3). Violence against press during post-election protests. https://rsf.org/en/news/violence-against-press-during-post-election-protests

Reporters Without Borders. (2010, August 2). Around 30 news media closed a few days ahead of presidential election. https://rsf.org/en/news/around-30-news-media-closed-few-days-ahead-presidential-election

Reporters Without Borders. (2014). 2014 World Press Freedom Index. https://rsf.org/en/world-press-freedom-index-2014

Reporters Without Borders. (2019a). Kenya: Steady decline in media freedom. Retrieved October 23, 2019, from https://rsf.org/en/kenya

Reporters Without Borders. (2019b). Uganda: Police raids cut short three radio interviews with opposition politician. Retrieved January 22, 2020, fromhttps://rsf.org/en/uganda-police-raids-cut-short-three-radio-interviews-opposition-politician

Reporters Without Borders. (2020a). Rwanda. Retrieved May 8, 2020, from https://rsf.org/en/rwanda

Reporters Without Borders. (2020b). Uganda. Retrieved June 3, 2020, from https://rsf.org/en/uganda

Reporters Without Borders. (2022a). Kenya. Retrieved December 12, 2022, from https://rsf.org/en/kenya

Reporters Without Borders. (2022b). Methodology used for compiling the World Press Freedom Index. https://rsf.org/en/index-methodologie-2022

Reporters Without Borders. (2022c). Rwanda. Retrieved January 7, 2023, from https://rsf.org/en/country/rwanda

Reporters Without Borders. (2022d). Uganda. Retrieved December 12, 2022, from https://rsf.org/en/uganda

Reporters Without Borders. (2022e). World Press Freedom Index. Retrieved December 11, 2022, from https://rsf.org/en/ranking

Repucci, S. (2019). Freedom and the media 2019: A downward spiral. Retrieved May 8, 2020, fromhttps://freedomhouse.org/report/freedom-media/freedom-media-2019

Reuters. (2021, January 17). Uganda's Museveni wins sixth term, rival alleges fraud. https://www.reuters.com/article/uk-uganda-election-idUSKBN29M04E

Reyntjens, F. (2017, July 11). Rwanda's election outcome is already decided. *African Arguments*. https://africanarguments.org/2017/07/11/rwanda-election-outcome-has-already-been-decided/

Rhodes, T. (2014, October 24). BBC's Rwanda documentary leads to illogical, illegal suspension. Committee to Protect Journalists. https://cpj.org/blog/2014/10/bbc-rwandan-documentary-leads-to-illogical-illegal.php

Rice, X. (2007, December 30). Kenyans riot as Kibaki declared poll winner. *The Guardian*. https://www.theguardian.com/world/2007/dec/31/kenya.topstories3

Rodny-Gumede, Y. (2015). Coverage of Marikana: War and conflict and the case for peace (journalism). *Social Dynamics, 41*(2), 359–374.

Run, P. (2014, February 1). *The Media in Transitional Democracies* by K. Voltmer [Book review]. *Media International Australia, Incorporating Culture & Policy,* 150, 199.

Russell, S. G. (2022, February 2). Gender equality in post-genocide Rwanda. UNESCO. Retrieved November 2, 2022, from https://world-education-blog.org/2017/01/19/gen der-equality-in-post-genocide-rwanda/

Rwanda Governance Board. (2021, November). Rwanda Media Barometer: The State of Media Development in Rwanda. https://www.rgb.rw/fileadmin/user_upload/RGB/ Publications/RWANDA_MEDIA_BAROMETER-RMB/RWANDA_MEDIA_BAR OMETER_2021.pdf

Rwanda Vision 2020. (2000, July). Republic of Rwanda, Ministry of Finance and Economic Planning. Retrieved June 7, 2020, from https://time.com/wp-content/uplo ads/2015/04/d402331a.pdf

Sang, H. (2015). Development discourse in Kenyan vernacular radio: A case study of Kass FM. *Research on Humanities and Social Sciences, 5*(6), 63–72.

Salih, M., & Markakis, J. (1998). *Ethnicity and the state in Eastern Africa.* Nordic Africa Institute.

Schneider, L. (2014). *Media freedom indices: What they tell us—and what they don't.* Deutsche Welle Akademie.

Seymore-Ure, C. (1974). *The political impact of mass media.* Constable.

Shea, S. (2002). The role of imperialism in Rwanda: Is colonialism dead? *Thought and Practice in African Philosophy,* 139–159. https://www.pdcnet.org/sixth-isaps/content/ sixth-isaps_2002_0139_0159

Siebert, F., Peterson, T., & Schramm, W. (1956). *Four theories of the press.* University of Illinois Press.

Silver, M. (2015, January 4). If you shouldn't call it the third world, what should you call it? NPR: Goats and Sodas. https://www.npr.org/sections/goatsandsoda/2015/01/04/ 372684438/if-you-shouldnt-call-it-the-third-world-what-should-you-call-it

Simiyu, T. F. (2013). Media ownership and framing in Kenya: A study of the ICC case against Uhuru Kenyatta. *Open Science Repository Communication and Journalism.* http://www.open-science-repository.com/media-ownership-and-framing-in-kenya-a-study-of-the-icc-case-against-uhuru-kenyatta.html

Simiyu, T. F. (2014). Media ownership and the coverage of the 2013 general election in Kenya: Democracy at the crossroads. *Global Media Journal: African Edition, 8*(1), 114–145.

Simon, S. (2019, November 16). Bobi Wine vs. Uganda's "dictator": It's "dangerous to sit down and resign to fate." NPR. https://www.npr.org/2019/11/16/780067936/bobi-wine-a-year-after-his-arrest-and-beating

Smith, D. (2012, July 25). The end of the west's humiliating affair with Paul Kagame. *The Guardian.* https://www.theguardian.com/world/2012/jul/25/paul-kagame-rwanda-us-britain

Sobel, M., & McIntyre, K. (2019). The state of journalism and press freedom in postgenocide Rwanda. *Journalism & Mass Communication Quarterly, 96*(2), 558–578.

Sobel Cohen, M., & McIntyre, K. (2020a). The state of press freedom in Uganda. *International Journal of Communication, 14,* 649–668.

Sobel Cohen, M., & McIntyre, K. (2020b). Local-language radio stations in Kenya: Helpful or harmful? *African Journalism Studies, 40*(3), 73–88.

Sobel Cohen, M., & McIntyre, K. (2021). Tweeter-in-chief: Rwandan president Paul Kagame's use of Twitter. *Journal of African Media Studies, 13*(1), 17–33.

Sommers, M. (2012). Stuck: Rwandan youth and the struggle for adulthood. University of Georgia Press.

Specia, M. (2017, April 15). How a nation reconciles after genocide killed nearly a million people. *New York Times.* https://www.nytimes.com/2017/04/25/world/africa/rwand ans-carry-on-side-by-side-two-decades-after-genocide.html

Ssenoga, G. (2018, October 8). How the Ugandan media has borne the brunt of censorship for decades. *The Wire.* https://thewire.in/world/how-the-ugandan-media-has-borne-the-brunt-of-censorship-for-decades

Ssuuna, I. (2016, October 10). Rwanda leader blasts France over 1994 plane crash inquiry. KSL.com. https://www.ksl.com/article/41802765/rwanda-leader-blasts-france-over-1994-plane-crash-inquiry

Straus, S. (2007). What is the relationship between hate radio and violence? Rethinking Rwanda's "radio machete." *Politics & Society, 35*(4), 609–637.

Straziuso, J. (2013, March 7). Kenya media self-censoring to reduce vote tension. *San Diego Union Tribune.* https://www.sandiegouniontribune.com/sdut-kenya-media-self-censoring-to-reduce-vote-tension-2013mar07-story.html

Stremlau, N. (2018). *Media, conflict, and the state in Africa.* Cambridge University Press.

Sundaram, A. (2014, March/April). Rwanda: The darling tyrant. *Politico.* https://www. politico.com/magazine/story/2014/02/rwanda-paul-kagame-americas-darling-tyr ant-103963

Sundaram, A. (2016). *Bad news: Last journalists in a dictatorship.* Penguin Random House.

Tabaire, B. (2007). The press and political repression in Uganda: Back to the future? *Journal of Eastern African Studies, 1*(2), 193–211.

Tangri, R., & Mwenda, A. M. (2008). Elite corruption and politics in Uganda. *Commonwealth & Comparative Politics, 46*(2), 177–194.

Taylor, C. C. (1999). *Sacrifice as terror: The Rwandan genocide of 1994.* Oxford University Press.

Thompson, A. (2019). Introduction. In A. Thompson (Ed.), *Media and mass atrocity: The Rwanda genocide and beyond* (pp. 1–16). McGill-Queens University Press.

Thomson, S. (2013). *Whispering truth to power: Everyday resistance to reconciliation in postgenocide Rwanda.* University of Wisconsin Press.

Thomson, S. (2014, May 1). Rwanda's National Unity and Reconciliation Program. *E-International Relations Journal.* https://www.e-ir.info/2014/05/01/rwandas-national-unity-and-reconciliation-program/

Thumim, N. (2012). *Self-representation and digital culture.* Palgrave Macmillan.

Tomaselli, K. G. (2011). (Afri)ethics, communitarianism and the public sphere. In N. Hyde-Clarke (Ed.), *Communication and media ethics in South Africa* (pp. 76–95). Juta.

Tripp, A. M. (2004). The changing face of authoritarianism in Africa: The case of Uganda. *Africa Today, 50*(3), 3–26.

Tucker, J. (2007). Enough! Electoral fraud, collective action problems, and post-communist colored revolutions. *Perspectives on Politics, 5*(3), 535–551.

Twaweza. (2021). World press freedom day 2021: Ugandan citizens' experiences and opinions on the media. https://twaweza.org/wp-content/uploads/2021/05/Media-WPFD-fact-sheet-d1.pdf

Uganda Bureau of Statistics. (2017). *Report of the national governance peace and security survey.* Uganda: Uganda Bureau of Statistics.

Uganda Business News. (2020, February 14). Circulation falls for Uganda newspapers in fourth quarter of 2019. Retrieved June 16, 2020, from https://ugbusiness.com/8425/circulation-falls-for-uganda-newspapers-in-fourth-quarter-of-2019

Uganda Communications Commission. (2020). List of authorized radio broadcasters as of 31st December 2020. Retrieved June 3, 2020, fromhttps://www.ucc.co.ug/wp-content/uploads/2021/01/FINAL-LIST-OF-AUTHORISED-RADIO-BROADCASTERS-AS-OF-31st-DECEMBER-2020.pdf

Ugangu, W. (2012). Normative media theory and the rethinking of the role of the Kenyan media in a changing social economic context. [Doctoral dissertation.] University of South Africa. https://uir.unisa.ac.za/bitstream/handle/10500/8606/thesis_ugangu_w.pdf?sequence=1&isAllowed=y

Ugangu, W. (2016). Kenya's difficult political transitions, ethnicity and the role of media. In L. L. Mukhongo & J. W. Macharia (Eds.), *Political influence of the media in developing countries* (pp. 12–24). Information Science Reference (an imprint of IGI Global).

UNESCO. (2018). Institute for statistics: Rwanda. Retrieved June 2, 2020, fromhttp://uis.unesco.org/en/country/rw

UNESCO. (2021). World trends in freedom of expression and media development: Global report 2021/2022. Retrieved October 18, 2022, fromhttps://www.unesco.org/reports/world-media-trends/2021/en

UNESCO. (2022). Journalism is a public good: World trends in freedom of expression and media development, global report 2021/2022. UNESCO. https://unesdoc.unesco.org/ark:/48223/pf0000379826

United Nations. (2018, January 26). General Assembly designates 7 April International Day of Reflection on 1994 genocide against Tutsi in Rwanda, amending title of annual observance. https://www.un.org/press/en/2018/ga12000.doc.htm

United Nations Security Council. (2016, March 7). Lord's Resistance Army. United Nations. https://www.un.org/securitycouncil/sanctions/2127/materials/summaries/entity/lord's-resistance-army

U.S. Department of State. (2021, March 30). *2020 Country Reports on Human Rights Practices: Rwanda.* Bureau of Democracy, Human Rights, and Labor. https://www.state.gov/reports/2020-country-reports-on-human-rights-practices/rwanda/

U.S. Department of State. (2021). 2021 Investment climate statements: Rwanda. Retrieved May 2, 2022, from https://www.state.gov/reports/2021-investment-climate-statements/rwanda/

Van de Walle, N. (2003). Presidentialism and clientelism in Africa's emerging party systems. *Journal of Modern African Studies, 41*(2), 297–321.

Verpoorten, M. (2005). Le coût en vies humaines du génocide rwandais: le cas de la province de Gikongoro [The cost in human lives of the Rwandan genocide: the case of the province of Gikongoro]. *Population, 60*(4), 331–367.

Voltmer, K. (2012). How far can media systems travel? Applying Hallin and Mancini's comparative framework outside the Western world. In D. C. Hallin & P. Mancini (Eds.), *Comparing media systems beyond the Western world* (pp. 96–118). Cambridge University Press.

Voltmer, K. (2013). *The media in transitional democracies.* Polity Press.

Voltmer, K., & Wasserman, H. (2014). Journalistic norms between universality and domestication: Journalists' interpretations of press freedom in six new democracies. *Global Media and Communication, 10*(2), 177–192.

Waldorf, L. (2007). Censorship and propaganda in post-genocide Rwanda. In A. Thompson (Ed.), *Media and the Rwanda genocide* (pp. 404–416). Pluto Press.

Walulya, G., & Nassanga, G. L. (2020). Democracy at stake: Self-censorship as a self-defence strategy for journalists. *Open Access Journal, 8*(1), 5–14. https://www.cogitat iopress.com/mediaandcommunication/article/view/2512

Wangui, J. J. (2014, March 13). Defence says Kenyan broadcaster called for Rift Valley peace. The Institute for War & Peace Reporting. https://iwpr.net/global-voices/defe nce-says-kenyan-broadcaster-called-rift-valley-peace

Wasserman, H. (2013). Journalism in a new democracy: The ethics of listening. *Communicatio, 39*(1), 67–84.

Wasserman, H. (2018). *Media, geopolitics, and power: A view from the global south.* University of Illinois Press.

wa Thiong'o, N. (1986). *Decolonising the mind: The politics of language in African literature.* East African Educational Publishers Ltd.

Weaver, D. (1998). *The global journalist: News people around the world.* Hampton Press.

Weaver, D., & Willnat, L. (2012). *The global journalist in the 21st century.* Routledge.

Whitehead, L. (2002). *Democratization: Theory and experience.* Oxford University Press.

Wilson, T., & Blood, D. (2019, August 12). Rwanda: Where even poverty data must toe Kagame's line. *Financial Times.* https://www.ft.com/content/683047ac-b857-11e9-96bd-8e884d3ea203

Wolfsfeld, G. (1997). *Media and political conflict: News from the Middle East.* Cambridge University Press.

World Bank. (2020a). Macro poverty outlook for Sub-Saharan Africa. Retrieved May 18, 2021, from https://www.worldbank.org/en/publication/macro-poverty-outlook/mpo_ssa

World Bank. (2020b). School enrollment, primary (% gross)—Rwanda. Retrieved November 6, 2021, from https://data.worldbank.org/indicator/SE.PRM.ENRR?locati ons=RW

World Bank. (2020c). Life expectancy at birth, total (years). Retrieved May 18, 2021, from http://data.worldbank.org/indicator/SP.DYN.LE00.IN

World Bank. (2021, June). Uganda secures $200 million to accelerate digital transformation and inclusiveness. Retrieved June 22, 2022, fromhttps://www.worldbank.org/en/news/press-release/2021/06/02/uganda-secures-200-million-to-accelerate-digital-tra nsformation-and-inclusiveness

Worldometer. (2020). Kenya population. Retrieved December 14, 2020, fromhttps://www.worldometers.info/world-population/kenya-population/

Xu, X. (2009). Development journalism. In K. Wahl-Jorgensen & T. Hanitzsch (Eds.), *The handbook of journalism studies* (pp. 357–370). Routledge.

Yanagizawa-Drott, D. (2014). Propaganda and conflict: Evidence from the Rwandan genocide. *Quarterly Journal of Economics, 129*(4), 1947–1994.

Yesil, M. M. (2014). The invisible threat for the future of journalism: Self-censorship and conflicting interests in an increasingly competitive media environment. *International Journal of Business and Social Science, 5*(3), 71–78.

Yoxon, B. (2017, November 30). Why elections don't always equal democracy: The case of Kenya. The Conversation. https://theconversation.com/why-elections-dont-always-equal-democracy-the-case-of-kenya-88341

Záhořík, J. (2012). Some notes on the failed decolonization of Rwanda. *West Bohemian Historical Review, 2*, 133–146.

Zakaria, F. (2009). Africa's new path: Paul Kagame charts a way forward. *New Presence: The Prague Journal of Central European Affairs, 11*(3), 7.

Zelizer, B. (2005). The culture of journalism. In J. Curran & M. Gurevitch (Eds.), *Mass media and society* (4th ed., pp. 198–214). Hodder Arnold.

Index

For the benefit of digital users, indexed terms that span two pages (e.g., 52–53) may, on occasion, appear on only one of those pages.

Tables are indicated by *t* following the page number